ME AND POVERTY

A Journey of Inspiration and Escape

Joseph Little

THE LITTLE PUBLISHING
C O M P A N Y

P.O. Box 91, Louisa, KY 41230

ISBN: 979-8-9987055-2-6 (Print Paperback)
ISBN: 979-8-9987055-1-9 (Print Hardcover)
ISBN: 979-8-9987055-0-2 (Ebook)

Library of Congress Control Number: 2025908104

Published by The Little Publishing Company

TABLE OF CONTENTS

FOREWORD

Some stories are meant to be told. Not just for the sake of the storyteller, but for the countless others who see pieces of themselves within the pages. This is one of those stories.

The journey through poverty is often described in statistics, policy debates, or charity appeals. But rarely do we get an honest, unfiltered glimpse into what it truly means to live it. To wrestle with it daily, to navigate the weight of limitation, and to fight for a future that looks different from the past. This book does just that.

The author does not simply recount hardship. He reveals the resilience, the self-discovery, and the quiet yet powerful acts of defiance against a cycle that threatened to consume him. This is not a tale of self-pity, nor is it an easy success story tied up with a neat bow. It is raw, unflinching, and, above all, real.

What makes this book extraordinary is its ability to challenge the reader. It is an invitation to look deeper, not just at poverty itself, but at the wounds it leaves behind. The choices made in the face of struggle. The ways we unknowingly sabotage ourselves. The moments of unexpected kindness that become lifelines.

But beyond the struggles, there is something greater at work. Even in the darkest moments, God never left. His presence can be seen in the resilience to keep going, in the hands that helped along the way, and in the hope that refused to die. This story is a reminder that no circumstance is greater than God's plan, no hardship too deep for His grace to reach, and no past too broken for Him to redeem. As you turn these pages, you are not just reading a story. You are stepping into a life. You are witnessing the battle between circumstance and willpower, between despair and hope, and ultimately, between fear and faith. And most importantly, you are reminded that breaking free is possible. It's not easy, not instant, but possible.

This book is more than a memoir. It is a testimony. It is proof that God's grace is present even in the hardest places. Most important, it is a call to action.

Read it with an open heart. It may just change the way you see the world, yourself, those struggling with poverty, and the God who walks with you through it all.

PREFACE

Dear Reader,

Poverty and I have had a rough relationship over the years. I kept trying to leave, but she had her hooks in me. I knew she was unhealthy. I knew I would regret letting her stay. I knew being seen with her would damage my reputation. Allowing her to linger in my life would keep me trapped under the same low ceiling that had crushed so many others before me. I knew all of this, but I loved her. Because when I had no one, I had poverty.

The relief she provided was always temporary. Like eating a bowl of ice cream only to step on the scale the next morning. Like staying up late, skipping class, and realizing too late that you have flunked out of college. The truth is, I had a relationship with poverty. It lasted for years. I wish I could say I was the only one affected by her, but the reality is she had infected many. In fact, this relationship lasted until a relationship with Jesus Christ countered it.

Read on to discover how I escaped this abusive relationship, broke the vicious cycle of poverty in my family, and ended up in the position to write this book.

Before diving in, I must acknowledge that many of the concepts in this book are not solely my own ideas. I can proudly say I have borrowed many of them from a life of gathered friends and mentors.

I am eternally grateful for the countless people who have invested in me from my youth to the present day. My teachers, pastors, friends, a few family members, entrepreneurs, business owners, and most importantly, my mentors. Each of them gave me a piece of themselves. They allowed me to glean the wisdom and guidance that ultimately led me to break up with poverty and step into a life of purpose.

PART ONE

THE JOURNEY

Chapter 1:

PERFECT PARENTS

L et me start by saying I am fully aware that perfect parents do not exist. Having a child of my own has only reinforced this truth. This chapter is not about longing for flawless parents or expecting something unattainable. It is about the reality of two parents who walked away.

Growing up in rural Appalachia in the 1980s, obtaining an education was not a given. For many, it was hardly expected, especially for those from families where education had never been a priority. My mother came from such a family, a long line of women who saw schooling as secondary to survival. She also came from a long line of women who had children young, as if it were an unspoken rite of passage.

For our family, the fact that my mother made it to the tenth grade was considered an accomplishment. It was further than most had gone. Mamaw often said that my mother was kind and that she had a soft heart. But she was also a troubled child.

From an early age, my mother struggled with fear, especially at night. She would hear voices, her paranoia growing stronger as the years went on. Eventually, she was diagnosed with schizophrenia and put on medication. But treatment was not a cure, and in her case, it was never a permanent solution. This is not the story of a woman who overcame every challenge, but neither is it the story of someone who didn't care. She was trapped in a battle she couldn't win, and as much as it hurt us, it must have hurt her too.

My mother had her first child, my oldest brother, when she was just sixteen. By then, she was already experimenting with drugs and alcohol, dipping her toes into a world that would soon consume her. Two years later, at eighteen, she had her second child. When my mother had her second child, she had already begun coming home to mamaw with needle marks on her arms. It was one of the first visible signs that what had once been occasional use was becoming something far worse.

With her mental illness compounding her struggles and no real support system to help her fight, she never really stood a chance.

One summer, when I was a teenager, our mother decided to take the boys and me school shopping. It wasn't something we did often, which made it feel significant. She wanted so badly to feel like she was providing, like she was capable of doing what mothers were supposed to do. So much so that she had saved most of the previous month's SSI checks, carefully holding onto them instead of spending impulsively as she often did. It was a rare moment of discipline, an effort to be the kind of mother she wished she could be. Her boyfriend was the one who drove us, and for that day, we were just a regular family going on an ordinary errand.

I was an older teen by then, just beginning to take an interest in weightlifting. There was something about it that fascinated me: the idea of making myself stronger, of building something solid and unshakable. Maybe I thought that if I could control my body, I could control the parts of my life that always felt so uncertain. Maybe I just liked the idea of becoming stronger than the circumstances that had always felt bigger than me.

When it came time to pick out clothes, I made a decision that felt bold in a way I could not fully explain. I spent a good portion of my clothing budget on a pair of weightlifting gloves. They weren't just gloves to me. They were a step toward something more, a small but tangible investment in the person I wanted to become. For once, I had chosen something not just because I needed it, but because I wanted it.

By the time we made it back to the car, I reached into the bag and immediately knew something was wrong. I rummaged through it, my movements growing more frantic, until reality hit me like a punch to the gut. One of the gloves was missing.

At first, I could not believe it. I checked the bag again and then again, as if sheer willpower could make it reappear. But it was gone, and the moment that realization settled in, everything inside me collapsed.

When you grow up in poverty, loss is never just loss. It carries a weight beyond the thing itself. It reminds you of what little you have, of how few chances you get. There is no room for carelessness, no space for mistakes. One wrong move, one moment of not paying attention, and something is gone forever. My mind immediately went to the worst places.

Of course, this happened to me. It wouldn't have happened to anyone else.

Of course, I wasted my money. I should have known better than to buy something I actually wanted.

I didn't deserve nice things.

Poverty teaches you to see the world in extremes. It is either all or nothing, success or failure, win or lose. There is no in-between, no second chances, no way to fix what is broken. You either get it right the first time, or you are left with nothing.

I didn't have the words for it back then, but later in life, I came across something that described this feeling perfectly. In The Mountain Is You, Brianna Wiest[1] explains how we often sabotage ourselves because, deep down, we don't believe we deserve more than what we've always known. We fear change, even if what we know is painful. That day, standing in the Walmart parking lot, I wasn't just upset about a missing glove. I was proving myself right. I had dared to want something, and this was my punishment for believing I could have it.

I was still spiraling when my mother's boyfriend spoke. His voice was calm, almost indifferent as if what he was saying was the simplest thing in the world.

"I'll go back inside and get you another pair."

I looked at him, stunned.

It was such a small gesture, but in my world, it was unheard of. No one replaced what was lost. No one offered second chances. No one went out of their way just because they could.

I have very few positive memories of my mother or the men in her life. But this one, this quiet moment of unexpected kindness, has never left me.

Mother Knows Best?

My collection of memories starts here. This is where the story of my childhood truly begins—not with warm bedtime stories or family traditions, but with social workers watching my mother closely, waiting for her to prove she could be the mother we needed. They gave her chance after chance, hoping she might pull it together, that she might fight to keep us. But she failed. Miserably.

When it became clear that we were going to be taken away for good, my mother had a final moment of what some might call "common sense." Instead of letting the system take us, she brought us to the only safety net she had left—her mother, our Mamaw. The plan, at least in her mind, was temporary. She would straighten things out, she said, and come back for us.

Although I was too young to remember with true clarity, the story has been told plenty enough in our family over the years. My father and mother drove us, my four brothers (at the time) and me, to our grandparents' house. They assured us it was just for a night. One night. They would be back in the morning. We clung to their words because we wanted to believe them.

Life with Mom had never been easy. It meant hunger. It meant mess. It meant a house so dirty that the filth became normal, the smell blending into the air until we no longer noticed. It meant never knowing when we'd eat next or if the water in the house would be working that day. It meant being unwashed, our skin caked with layers of neglect we were too young to recognize as anything unusual.

But then, we stepped into our grandparents' home, and for the first time, we experienced something we hadn't even known to wish for—cleanliness.

Mamaw, didn't waste a moment. She and my grandfather gathered us up, one by one, and ran warm baths. Not the quick, barely-there kind we were used to, but real baths, filled with soapy water that bubbled and foamed. I remember the feeling of it, how the dirt lifted off my skin, how the scent of the soap was so unfamiliar that it almost felt wrong. But then we started laughing, splashing, marveling at the strange, slippery sensation of our own clean skin. It was something so simple, yet it felt like stepping into another world.

Then the next morning came.

And she wasn't there.

A day turned into two. Then three. By the end of the week, the truth settled in, heavy and undeniable. Mom wasn't coming back.

The phone call came a few days later. Mamaw answered, and we all watched, waiting, hoping. But it was just confirmation of what we had already begun to understand.

She wasn't capable of being the mother we needed. Whether she gave up or was simply overwhelmed by forces beyond her control, I'll never fully know.

And just like that, Mamaw, at forty-eight years old, found herself taking on a responsibility she hadn't planned for. Five children of her own had already passed through her hands, and now, she had five more boys to raise. I often wonder if, in that moment, she hesitated. If she silently asked herself whether this was the biggest mistake of her life.

Because, for better or worse, our lives were now in her hands.

Note that after they left us with our grandparents, my parents didn't walk away from each other immediately. Their relationship was messy, full of breakups and reconciliations that never seemed to last. My mother would leave, get involved with another one of my brothers' fathers, and find her way back to my dad. It was a cycle that repeated itself for years.

During that time, mamaw did what she could to keep some connection between us and our parents. She arranged visits, hoping that if we saw them enough, the distance wouldn't feel so final. For a while, it worked. They would show up, sometimes together, sometimes apart, giving us just enough presence to keep us hoping things might change.

But they never did. The spiral continued, and the visits became fewer. My father, who had always seemed like he was halfway out the door, finally made his exit. Around the time I turned ten, he moved to Virginia for good. After that, he was no longer someone I saw. He was just a voice on the phone, distant and fading, a presence that barely felt real.

Being from Martin County, Kentucky, it was not unusual to come from a broken home or to be raised in poverty. Eastern Kentucky had long been a symbol of rural hardship, a place where struggle was passed down like an heirloom. President Lyndon B. Johnson highlighted this reality in 1964 when he stood on the front porch of a Martin County resident's home and declared his War on Poverty. Looking at the families struggling around him, he said, "This administration today, here and now, declares unconditional war on poverty in America."[2] His words carried weight at the time, but for families like mine, change didn't come fast enough.

Our situation was even more difficult because we weren't just poor; we were also living in a home that was constantly falling apart, both physically and emotionally. My mother kept me until I was four and my oldest brother until he was ten, but the places we lived in could hardly be called homes. We weren't just struggling financially; we were surviving in conditions no child should have to endure. The walls around us may have stood, but they did nothing to keep out the cold of neglect or the storm of addiction that raged inside.

My mother battled schizophrenia, but instead of getting the help she needed, she abused her medication, slipping further into a world where reality blurred. My father chose his own escape. Rather than raising his only son, he spent his time and money on marijuana, numbing himself to responsibilities he never wanted. Stability was something we never knew. Love, as most children understood it, was something we had only seen in glimpses.

Out of five boys, we all shared one mother but had four different fathers. Even now, when I say those words out loud, I can't help but think of the woman at the well in the Bible. The one Jesus met and spoke to with both kindness and brutal honesty, despite her past. My mother's life was far from perfect, and so was ours. We weren't the ideal family with two parents, two kids, a house with a white picket fence, and a dog in the yard. We were something else entirely—something messy, complicated, and uncertain.

At the time, I couldn't see it, but God was looking far beyond what I understood.

Child Protective Services typically keeps a case open for six months, giving the mother a chance to turn her life around. Mamaw was granted temporary custody at first, just until Mom could prove she was capable of raising us. But that never happened. Mom refused to cooperate. Maybe she tried in her own way, but her struggles with addiction and mental illness made it impossible for her to succeed. No matter how much she may have wanted to be a good mother, she was drowning in a battle she couldn't win. Instead, she told Mamaw and the court they could keep us.

At the time, it felt like just another rejection, another reminder that we weren't worth fighting for. But looking back, I see it differently. It was a blessing. As much as we had already endured, the truth is, we were lucky to have made it out alive.

There was a house fire. Actually, there were a few. Flames licking at the walls, smoke curling into every crevice, the thick scent of burning wood and fabric filling the air. Fires weren't an uncommon sight in homes like ours, where neglect met misfortune at every turn. I was too young to remember this particular fire, but Mamaw told it to me vividly.

I had been left outside on the porch, the heat of the flames warming my small face as I watched my mother run for safety. She didn't look back, not at first. My tiny hands gripped the wooden railing, my cries lost in the chaos. In her defense, she did eventually return for me. I suppose that counts for something.

Her history of neglect didn't stop there. There was the time my brother and I were left on a church bus, waiting for a mother who never came. Maybe she thought we were in good hands. Maybe she just didn't think at all. The filth of our home was one thing, but the uncertainty of our next meal was another. Hunger became an unwanted companion, always lurking, always gnawing. We learned quickly that food wasn't promised, that empty stomachs were just part of life. These are just a few details to help you understand why social services intervened.

The day she dropped us off at Mamaw's, my father was with her. It was a moment that would define the rest of my life.

I don't know what went through his mind that day. I don't know if he hesitated, if he wondered for even a second whether he should stay. All I know is that he chose to walk away.

He decided that day that he would not be a father.

Not the kind that helps with homework. Not the kind that gives dating advice or teaches his son how to be a man. Not the kind that sits in the stands at ball games, clapping and cheering. Not the kind that holds his child and says, *I'm proud of you.*

He decided not to feed. Not to hug. Not to give forehead kisses.

Not to teach me how to ride a bike or tie my shoes.

Not to attend my wedding. Not to be there for my college or graduate school graduation.

Not to see the birth of his grandson.

Not to witness me rise above the poverty that had swallowed so many before me.

A father is supposed to do all these things. Mine chose not to.

And yet, there was something almost admirable about the way he left. He gave me a clean break. He vanished.

I could respect that.

He knew he was unfit, and instead of weaving in and out of my life, leaving behind a trail of broken promises and confusion, he disappeared. There was no false hope, no waiting by the door, no questioning whether this time would be different. Besides an occasional phone call and a couple of summer stays we will discuss later, he was gone, and that was that.

Mom, on the other hand, kept things messy.

She would come around occasionally, mostly on her birthday or the holidays. Not because she missed us, but because she wanted to be loved and admired. We all want that, I suppose. The trouble was, she was almost always under the influence.

She wanted the joy of motherhood without the weight of responsibility. She wanted love without sacrifice.

But love doesn't work like that.

Every time she reappeared, she reopened wounds that barely had time to scab over. Every visit was a reminder that she could have chosen differently but didn't. She kept damaging the relationship, never allowing space for healing.

Unlike Dad, who left cleanly, she made sure her absence was felt in the most painful way possible, by being just close enough for us to hope but never close enough to stay.

There was one holiday when Mamaw had finally had enough. She took one look at our mother—unkempt, unsteady, a shadow of the woman she should have been—and told her to leave. For the first time, she refused to let us boys see her in such poor condition.

I think Mamaw knew, deep down, that every visit did more harm than good. Nearly every encounter with our mother felt like an obligation, a forced hug to a stranger who happened to share our blood. Because that's what she was—a stranger.

And yet, biblically speaking, we are taught to honor our mother and father, no matter what. So we did.

We hugged a woman we barely knew a couple of times a year. We muttered *I love you* without meaning it. How could we? Love requires connection, and she had severed that long ago.

Those hugs carried more than just emptiness. They carried the overwhelming stench of body odor, the consequence of living without electricity or running water. They carried the discomfort of knowing that within days, our heads would be shaved to rid us of the lice she unknowingly brought with her.

I don't share these stories for pity. I made it out. I survived. But I know there are others who are still living this reality.

If you're reading this, you might know a child just like that.

They could be sitting in your classroom today, quiet and withdrawn. They could be in your church tonight, nodding off from exhaustion. They could be on your football field this Friday, pushing through the pain with a determination that no one understands.

Coaches, pastors, counselors, teachers, and parents, I urge you to take a moment to look a little deeper and show genuine compassion. Behind every child's smile, every word they speak, and every action they take, there may be a story you're unaware of—a story of hardship, fear, or silent struggles they face at home. The weight they carry, though invisible, can be overwhelming.

Sometimes, they don't have the words to express what's wrong, or perhaps they've learned to hide their pain behind a mask of normalcy. But one simple act of kindness, a listening ear, or even a smile can mean more than you might realize. It can be the very thing that helps them hold on when everything around them feels uncertain.

Remember, your empathy and understanding could be the spark of hope that a child desperately needs. What may seem small to you can make a world of difference in their lives.

Summers With Dad

I was sixteen, caught between boyhood and something that vaguely resembled adulthood. For the past year, my birth father had been calling me every couple of days. It was strange at first, hearing his voice more regularly after years of scattered, inconsistent check-ins. He never had much to say, never asked the deep questions a father might ask a son he had been absent from for so long. But he called, and that had to count for something.

Most of our conversations felt like a performance. I was the one carrying them, steering them forward so they didn't fizzle out into silence. I filled the gaps with stories, making sure I sounded impressive. I told him about my grades, how hard I had been working out, and the girls I had been "dating." Every word was deliberate. If I could just say the right things, maybe he'd hear something in my voice that made him proud. Maybe he'd finally see me. Maybe, just maybe, he'd stick around this time.

The school year was coming to a close when he asked something I never saw coming.

"Son, would you like to come spend the summer with me and Kelly?"

His voice was casual, as if this was the most normal thing in the world.

It caught me off guard, but it wasn't the first time he had asked me to spend a summer with him. When I was 12, I stayed a few weeks with him. That time, my older brother was with me. The same brother I had once carried when he was too weak to walk. Having him there made all the difference. Back then, I wasn't alone in trying to understand my father's world. This time, I would be.

Kelly was his wife at the time, my stepmother. I barely knew her. Then again, I barely knew him. He had always been a distant figure in my life, checking in just enough to remind me he existed but never enough to feel like a real father. He abandoned me when I was four, disappearing into his own life without so much as an apology. There was no explanation, no sit-down conversation where he told me why he left. Just silence, and then, years later, phone calls that tried to bridge the gap but never quite did.

The crazy part? I wasn't angry. I probably should have been, but I wasn't. I had spent so much time convincing myself that I didn't need him, that I was fine without him, that I never stopped to question if it was actually true. Maybe I just wanted to understand him.

Maybe I wanted to see for myself if there was even the slightest chance we could build something resembling a normal father-son relationship.

So, I said yes.

After what felt like endless begging, my grandparents finally gave in and agreed to let me spend the summer in Virginia. It had taken some convincing, but I wasn't surprised that Mamaw was the one who ultimately caved. Out of all the so-called fathers we had, she always had a soft spot for mine. Maybe it was because when I was younger, he was the one who showed up the most. Or maybe it was because, out of everyone, he had treated my mother with the most respect, even when she was at her most fragile.

The moment I got the green light, my father wasted no time. He made the five-hour drive from Floyd, Virginia, to Floyd County, Kentucky. I didn't technically live in Floyd County. I was from the neighboring county of Martin, but this was how I had always placed him on a map. Floyd to Floyd. Fairly close, yet worlds apart.

When he arrived, he spent a few hours catching up with my family, reintroducing himself in the way that people who disappear and reappear tend to do. He introduced Kelly, my stepmother, and the whole thing felt surreal. For so long, he had been a voice on the other end of the phone, someone I tried to hold onto through conversations that never lasted long enough. And now, here he was, standing in my grandparents' living room, shaking hands and exchanging pleasantries like a relative who had simply been away for a while.

Then, just like that, we were off.

For months, I had imagined what it would be like to spend real time with my father, to have an actual summer with him instead of just hearing his voice through a receiver. And now, it was happening. The entire drive back, I couldn't stop talking. I had so many plans, so many things I wanted to do together. Fishing trips, grilling in the backyard, maybe even camping. I imagined us sitting on a porch, swapping stories, making up for lost time like something out of a movie.

When we finally pulled into his driveway, I took it all in. His house was small, almost tucked away in the middle of nowhere, and I loved it instantly. It was the kind of place that felt like it had a story, maybe even a few secrets. The forest surrounding it was completely flat, the ground covered in a thick layer of pine needles.

Even now, years later, I can still picture it. The scent of the trees, the way the branches swayed lazily in the breeze, the eerie quiet that settled over everything. And the basement. That basement felt like something out of a horror novel. The kind of place you'd avoid at night, even if you didn't believe in ghosts.

But none of that mattered. This was my father's home, and for the first time in my life, I was going to be a part of it.

Dad had recently lost his job at Hardee's after supposedly hurting his back unloading a food delivery truck. To me, that meant one thing. I'd get to spend all day with him while Kelly was at work. That was supposed to be the silver lining, the whole reason I came here. But every morning, without fail, I woke up to an empty house.

Dad had always struggled with insomnia. He was usually up before the sun, pacing the house or smoking on the porch, lost in his thoughts. But where did he go every morning? That was the question that started to eat at me. Whenever I asked, his answers were vague and dismissive.

"Ah, just gonna go help a friend with some work and earn a few dollars."

"Just heading into town for a bit."

That was it. No details, no invitation for me to come along. And that was the part that didn't sit right with me. I had left home, packed up my entire summer, just to be here, to finally build something with my father. Yet, most days, he was gone before I even had the chance to see him.

After weeks of pushing and making it clear that I wasn't letting this go, he finally let me tag along. At first, nothing seemed unusual. Most of the time, we visited family members I had never met before. Distant cousins, old aunts and uncles, people whose names blurred together. It was the first time I truly got to learn about my Indian heritage, and I soaked up every story they told.

One visit, in particular, stood out. My aunt, who lived in a weathered single-wide trailer, had covered every inch of her walls with Indian arrowheads. She spoke with pride, telling me about each one as I ran my fingers over their smooth, cool surfaces. It was fascinating, a glimpse into a history I had never been given access to before.

But then, I noticed something.

Dad was gone.

It wasn't unusual at this point. Every visit seemed to follow the same pattern. We'd arrive together, he'd make small talk, and then, at some point, he'd slip away. When I eventually found him, he'd be in another part of the house, leaning in close, whispering to whoever we were visiting.

At first, I convinced myself it was nothing. Maybe they were just catching up. Maybe I was overthinking it. But then came the exchanges. A few words hushed between them, a quick glance in my direction, and then something being passed between hands. Small, discreet, like they had done it a thousand times before.

It didn't take long to realize that my father struggled with self-medicating and that it was a problem. It wasn't just something he did. It was something that consumed him. Every decision, every dollar, every plan seemed to revolve around it.

The car was always on empty. Rather than putting in enough gas to get through the day, he'd scrape together just enough. $1.10 here, maybe a little more there. Just enough to make it to whoever was selling to him. In the entire two months I spent in Virginia, I don't think I ever saw the gas gauge rise above "E."

Dad and Kelly shared that one car. Every morning, against her wishes, he'd drop Kelly off at work, and from there, the day was his. He'd spend it driving from place to place, buying, borrowing, doing whatever it took to get his next fix. Meanwhile, Kelly was left wondering if she'd even have a ride home or if she'd have to call her mother to come get her.

The fights between them were constant. Kelly would scream. He'd shut down. Then she'd storm out, swearing she was done. Some nights, she'd be gone for hours. Other times, she wouldn't come back until the next day, her mother dropping her off at the house with the same tired look on her face.

And then there were the worst nights. The ones where the arguments weren't about the car or the money but about something far more basic. The nights when Kelly, voice tight with frustration, would ask, "Where is our next meal coming from?" The occasional leftovers that Kelly would bring home from her shift at Hardees would only go so far.

Dad never had an answer.

That summer in Virginia opened my eyes in ways I never expected. My father cared about me. I could see that. He wanted to be a good dad, but he didn't know how and still hold onto his addiction. In the end, he chose the latter.

One afternoon, while we were out running one of his usual errands, he offered me a chance to smoke something he'd picked up recently. The words hung between us for a moment before I shook my head and told him no. Something shifted after that. The air between us grew heavier. It wasn't anger or disappointment, just a quiet understanding that we were standing on opposite sides of a line we could never cross together.

From that day forward, I stopped looking at him as a father. He became more like a friend I was stuck on vacation with. The rest of the summer blurred into a cycle of playing the same few Nintendo 64 games, rewatching early 2000s TV shows on scratched-up DVDs, and listening to Dad and Kelly fight over the same things, over and over again.

Dysfunction seemed to follow me wherever I went. It was stitched into my childhood, embedded in the people around me, and woven into every home I stepped into. But that summer gave me something I didn't even realize I needed—closure.

God had shown me, clear as day, what I was meant to leave behind. And for that, I would always be grateful.

Exodus 20:12(KJV): "Honor your father and your mother, that your days may be long upon the land which the Lord your God is giving you."

Chapter 2:

A HOUSE, BUT NOT A HOME

Although our grandparents could provide us with shelter and cleanliness, they could not provide much more. When we first arrived, they had no formal income, only food stamps. This was something that weighed on my grandfather day in and day out. By the age of forty-five, my grandparents were on a fixed income. My grandfather received a small disability check due to an old mining accident that had crushed his back, leaving him unable to do hard labor. Belle, my mamaw, had never held a tax-paying job in her life. She had spent her years raising children, scraping by, doing what she could to survive.

Every day, my grandfather would gather just enough herbs from the hills to sell and then buy a gallon of milk or a loaf of bread. The closest grocery store was a thirty-minute drive away, but the cost of gas meant that unless it was a special occasion, whatever the gas station had would have to do. I remember nights when dinner consisted of nothing but a slice of white bread soaked in watered-down gravy, and we ate it like it was a feast because we knew no better.

For those who have never set foot in the hills of Appalachia, they are both beautiful and brutal. Towering trees and rolling landscapes hide deep poverty, isolation, and struggle. Some roads wind so steeply they seem to disappear into the clouds. There are places where the land remains untouched, places where nature rules and man survives only by knowing its rhythms. For my grandfather, those hills were both his refuge and his burden.

Herbing was honest work, and thankfully, it was lonely work too. It gave him a reason to escape the chaos of a house suddenly filled with children he never expected to raise. But the weight of it all never left his shoulders.

To truly understand what life was like under my grandfather's roof, you have to understand the man himself. He was not my biological grandfather. After my real grandfather passed, mamaw remarried. And this man, the one who raised us, was the only grandfather I had ever known.

He was a man shaped by hardship, carrying wounds that never fully healed. His childhood had been nothing short of tragic—marked by abuse so severe that most people wouldn't be able to stomach the details. He had lived through things no child should ever endure. And like a shadow that refuses to fade, that trauma followed him throughout his life, slipping into his parenting, his discipline, and the way he saw the world. He never fully escaped it, even when he had children of his own, even when he had us.

He and my rebellious older brother were constantly at odds. It seemed that every conversation between them ended in shouting, cursing, or even more common, physical fights. Their tempers clashed like flint and steel, sparking fires that no one could put out. I remember one fight in particular, though I wish I didn't. My grandfather, his face red with anger, grabbed a broomstick and pressed it against my brother's throat as he lifted him off the ground. The veins in his arms bulged as he held him there, eyes filled with something between rage and desperation. My brother struggled, gasping, but he never cried out. He never begged. He never would. The memory of it still burns, a scene too painful to forget.

I lost count of how many times my brother stormed out of the house, swearing that this time he was never coming back. But he always did. Sometimes hours later, sometimes days. My grandfather would get the police involved if he were gone too long, forcing my brother to return home.

Looking back now, I see my grandfather as a man caught between two lives. He had lived through his own childhood nightmare, he had already done his part by raising his own children into adulthood, and was ready to live out the rest of his days in quiet. He had found someone new, a partner in my mamaw, and had every right to expect some peace. But instead, life handed him five boys he didn't know, five extra mouths to feed, and a new kind of struggle he never saw coming.

The financial stress ate away at him, pressing down like the weight of those Appalachian hills. But no matter how heavy the burden, there was one thing stronger, his love for mamaw. He would do anything to make her happy, even if it meant breaking himself in the process.

As we grew older, the struggle to provide became even more obvious. We started noticing things, how our clothes never seemed to fit right, how the other kids at school had new shoes while we wore the same pair until the soles peeled away. Hand-me-downs were passed down again and again, shirts worn threadbare, jeans patched and re-patched. When you're little, you don't care. You run barefoot, play in the dirt, make do. But when you get older, when you start wanting to fit in, that's when it stings. That's when shame settles into your bones.

And as our shame grew, so did my grandfather's resentment.

You really couldn't blame the man. Keeping food on the table alone was grueling work, but when you added in the stress of making ends meet on nothing more than a disability check and some food stamps, it was unbearable. He and Mamaw were uneducated. They had never learned about savings accounts or financial planning. In our house, money was managed with a ten-cent spiral notebook and a checkbook, nothing more. Every day, my grandfather would sit hunched over that notebook, flipping through pages, and counting pennies.

His fingers traced over numbers, trying to stretch what little we had just one more day.

Mamaw carried just as much weight, though hers was different. She had her own struggles and mental health battles that no one understood, let alone talked about. There were times when it got too much for her, when she had to break and reset. But she never gave up. Not once. No matter how exhausted, how overwhelmed, she always came back to doing the one thing she knew, providing.

And somehow, in all that struggle, there were still moments of joy.

Some of my happiest childhood memories came from watching Mamaw cook. She could make a meal out of almost nothing, and to us, it was magic. She taught us how to roll dough and how to stretch a meal so that no one went hungry. Her staples became our comfort. The occasional doughnuts made from canned biscuits, deep-fried and dusted with powdered sugar were what dreams are made of. Pan after pan of cornbread, golden and warm. One of our favorites, though most wouldn't believe it, was a thick slice of cornbread covered in a generous layer of ketchup, a poor man's dessert that, to us, tasted like heaven.

But no matter how tempting, Mamaw never let us skip straight to the sweet stuff. We had to eat our main meal first, usually soup beans or spaghetti, the kind of meals that could be stretched across days.

Often, we leaned heavily into our Appalachian heritage with one of our staple meals—chicken and dumplings. The process of preparing it was brutal, yet, for most of my family, strangely entertaining.

We always had a steady supply of well-fed chickens on our property, though I despised them. There was rarely a day when I didn't step in chicken poop, and as someone with a strong aversion to germs, it made my skin crawl. But my brothers? They loved the whole process, from start to finish.

It would begin with Mamaw selecting the best-looking chickens, the ones she thought would make the best meal. Then came the part I dreaded most—our grandfather would grab the unfortunate bird, grip it tight, and with his bare hands, and twist it until its head snapped clean off. My brothers found a twisted sort of joy in watching the headless chickens flail, running around in frantic circles until their bodies finally gave out.

Once they stopped moving, someone would roll up some newspapers to create a torch, scorching the exposed neck before Mamaw took over. She always had a giant pot of boiling water ready, and the birds would be submerged just long enough to loosen the feathers. That's when we, the unwilling volunteers, were called into action.

The chickens were still hot as we worked to pluck them clean, the stench of damp feathers filling the air. I tried to focus on the task, but the smell turned my stomach every time. Just when we thought we were finished, Grandfather would light another torch to burn off the tiny hairs that remained before passing them off to the kitchen, where Mamaw would work her magic.

Despite the chaos of our lives, she always said I was the quiet one. The others acted up and got into trouble, but my problem, she said, was different—I was always crying for my parents.

Nights were the worst. Maybe it was something I had inherited from my mother, who also struggled with the dark, but as soon as the lights went out, fear crept in. No matter how much we had been neglected, there was still an instinct, a desperate longing to be loved, to be held. I vividly remember waking from nightmares, heart pounding, breath shaky, and running to my grandparents' bedroom for comfort.

But comfort never came.

If my grandfather found me, I was scolded and immediately ordered to go back to my own bed. I would stand there in the doorway, tears streaming down my face, begging, pleading.

"You won't even know I'm here," I whispered once. "Please, just let me sleep at the edge of the bed... at your feet."

But the answer was always the same.

"Go on now. Get."

And so, night after night, I turned around, wiping my tears as I made my way back to the cold, bed that never felt warm, welcoming, or like mine. This was probably because it was always shared by a couple of brothers stealing blankets.

Deep Compassion

I was always a deeply compassionate child. I felt things too much, too strongly. I would cry over simple things, whether it was a sad story, a harsh word, or just the weight of emotions I didn't understand. At first, I thought it was a gift, something that made me different in a good way. Allowed me to have compassion for others. But in my family, sensitivity wasn't seen as a gift. It was seen as weakness.

I became an easy target. At school, the kids bullied me for it. At home, my brothers joined in. Even my uncles took their turn. They saw my tears as something to exploit, a form of entertainment. It wasn't just teasing—it was deliberate. They would poke and prod, finding new ways to push me, waiting to see how long it would take for me to break. And when I did, when the tears finally came, they would laugh in my face.

I never understood how grown men could be so unhappy with their own lives that they found joy in breaking a child. It wasn't just cruelty. It was a game. They would see how far they could go, how upset they could make me, then turn around and yell at me when I finally reacted. If I got angry, if I lashed out, they would act like I was the problem. Like I was the one out of control. It was a cycle I couldn't escape.

I wished I had a father who was different. Not just one who was physically present, but one who saw me, who understood me, who knew how to help me through it. I wished I had a father who would sit down with me, talk to me, and teach me how to handle emotions instead of treating them like something shameful. I guess you could say I just wanted someone to protect me as a kid. But it never happened. Instead, I had men who laughed at my pain, and made sure I knew that crying only made things worse.

For most of my life, I learned to suppress. I learned to hold everything in because showing emotion meant opening myself up to more torment. I clenched my jaw so hard, so often, that I ended up with stress fractures in my teeth. Tears became my only outlet, my only way to stop myself from screaming. I would shut a door slowly, carefully, because slamming it would only bring more attention and trouble. Then I would grit my teeth so tightly that it felt like my head might split open, trying to contain everything inside me—anger, sadness, frustration, confusion. Unfortunately, like many other kids from similar home lives, these emotions eventually escalated into thoughts of harming myself.

I spent a lot of time angry at God. I couldn't understand why I had to come from this family, why my parents didn't want me, why I was stuck in a life where no one showed me the kind of love I so desperately needed. I never stopped wanting it. I never stopped hoping for it.

Yes, I admit I was different. I was a thinker. I was someone who felt things deeply, and carried emotions close to the surface. Even now, as a professional, I still wear my heart on my sleeve, though I've learned some hard lessons because of it. Experience has taught me that not everyone has your best interest at heart, even if you have theirs. Some people take advantage of kindness. Some see vulnerability as an opportunity rather than something to be respected.

My brothers and I shared a struggle—we were all abandoned. That was our common ground, the wound we all carried. I had hoped that would be enough to pull us together, to make us stronger as a unit. I wanted us to lean on each other, to figure out how to fill the hole in our hearts together. But that never happened. We were too different, too disconnected.

As mentioned earlier, from a young age I felt God had given me a gift. The ability to truly share in people's pain, to comfort them in ways that went beyond just words. It wasn't just about knowing what to say or what to do. Sometimes, it was as simple as sitting with someone in their grief, letting them know they weren't alone. A look of understanding, a shared tear, a quiet moment of solidarity.

Some would say I grew up too sensitive. That I felt too much, cared too much. And maybe that's true. I had a lot of lonely, scary nights, nights when the weight of everything felt unbearable. My brothers and I never grew close the way I had hoped. Our interests were too different, and our ways of coping were too far apart.

Looking back, I realize that while I had this deep connection to the struggles of others, I lacked the emotional intelligence to handle my own. I didn't know how to process my feelings, or how to regulate them in a way that made sense. I understood pain—I just didn't know what to do with my own.

God's Love

I discovered God's love at a very young age. I remember realizing, in my own childlike way, the depth of love and affection Jesus had for us. I grew up in church, hearing about it all the time. It was something I held onto, something that felt safe, even when everything else didn't.

In school, though, I struggled to understand why not everyone had that same love inside them. If Jesus taught kindness and compassion, why didn't people live by it? Why did some kids choose to be so ruthless, to go out of their way to hurt others? I couldn't comprehend how someone could find joy in tormenting another person, especially someone who had done nothing to them. What was the satisfaction of making someone cry? Why kick someone lying in a fetal position who only ever treated you with kindness?

That confusion only deepened at home. As I've mentioned, my whole family seemed to enjoy watching me cry—brothers, grandparents, uncles, cousins. It was as if my tears were some kind of entertainment, like a show they couldn't get enough of. My uncles, in particular, took it to another level. They would actually take pictures of me crying so they could laugh about it later. The cruelty of it all was something I could never wrap my head around, especially on Sundays when those same people would sit in church and hear about God's love. They would nod along, pretending they had it in their hearts, but I knew the truth. Their actions spoke louder than any sermon.

On top of it all, I had a severe case of eczema that plagued me throughout my childhood. It covered my body, but my hands were the worst. My fingers would be covered in hundreds of tiny blisters—painful, itchy, burning. It happened often and there was no relief. The itch was unbearable, especially between my fingers. It felt like chickenpox mixed with poison ivy, a sensation that never seemed to stop.

It wasn't until college that I discovered the simplest of solutions. The breakouts, the pain, the years of suffering—it all could have been avoided if I had just known to lotion my hands. Something so small, something no one had ever bothered to teach me, had made my childhood that much harder.

The vicious cycle of my eczema was predictable but no less unbearable each time. It would start with weeks of relentless itching, the kind that woke me up multiple times a night. Then, the blisters would swell, merging into one another until they finally burst and dried out. I knew this was only the beginning. The worst was yet to come.

Phase three was always the hardest. My hands would split open, raw and bleeding from the slightest movement. Even bending a finger would send sharp, stinging pain through my skin. But I never let it stop me from playing basketball on our little dirt court. I would dribble with bloodied hands, leaving faint red prints on the ball. It wasn't just a game to me; it was my escape. It was therapy, a way to forget the pain, if only for a little while.

The final stages were scabbing and, at last, peeling. I used to think about how incredible it was that our bodies could regenerate like that. As kids, we would smear Elmer's glue on our hands just to let it dry and peel it off. That was my reality every few months— except there was no glue. The flaky skin would lift away on its own, revealing fresh, untouched skin underneath. It was the only moment of relief I ever got before the cycle inevitably started over.

I craved normalcy. I wanted to be like everyone else, to have hands that didn't constantly burn and itch. Hands that didn't crack open just from being used. My whole family was aware of my condition, but that didn't mean they treated it with kindness. One night, when I was around twelve, my uncle decided to make me the punchline of one of his jokes.

I sat there, miserable, trying not to scratch the burning itch between my fingers when he looked at my blistered hands and said, "Oh, that? Yeah, I had the same thing at your age. I know how to fix it, but you're not gonna like it."

Desperate for relief, I latched onto his words. "I'll do whatever it takes."

He proceeded to tell me that the only way to cure it was to expose all the blisters to fresh air. And how else could I do that, he asked, except with a rugged kitchen knife? His voice was so convincing. "You have to scrape open all the blisters," he explained, "and before they close back up, you pour rubbing alcohol over them. After that, you'll never deal with it again."

I trusted him. Just like I had trusted my family my entire life, despite the many times they had let me down. I followed his instructions as he sliced through the blisters, gritting my teeth through the pain. And then, when he was done, he laughed.

He laughed!

He never had eczema. He never suffered the way I had. He made it all up just to see if I'd go through with it. I remember the way he looked at me, amused, as I sat there in pain, realizing I had been tricked.

That was the moment something shifted in me. He was just another person I had put my trust in, and he had let me down. Just like my mom, my dad, my older brothers, and grandfather-who I had desperately wanted to have a relationship with but never could.

Eventually, I stopped letting people in.

Stolen Potential

At this point, you might be wondering about my brothers. Were they suffering the same abuse as I was? And if so, why did they join in? The answer is complicated. We all started in the same place, a run-down house in Meathouse, attending a Baptist church that sat near a literal dump.

The house itself wasn't much better. Over time, it became infested with snakes. Not just one or two, but enough that it no longer felt like our home. My family finally decided to move, and we ended up in a single-wide trailer on Blacklog. It was there, in that narrow space, that my brother's life changed forever.

We had cousins who lived just across the road, and at eight years old, my older brother spent most of his days running back and forth between our house and theirs. It was routine. Safe, even, in the way that kids believe their world is safe—until one day it wasn't.

That day, my brother was kicking a can along the road, lost in his own little game, his head down as he made his way across. He never saw the truck. A full-sized Dodge, barreling toward him at over 60 miles per hour in a 45-zone. The driver never saw him either. By the time the brakes screamed against the pavement, it was already too late.

The impact sent my brother flying 20 feet from where his shoes remained.

I didn't see it happen. None of us did. We only heard it—the sickening thump of metal meeting flesh, the tires skidding against the asphalt, and then the smell. The terrible, burning smell of rubber scorched into the road.

Ambulances arrived, sirens wailing, followed closely by the police. Red and blue lights flickered against our mobile home windows. Vehicle after vehicle cast shadows over the stretch of road where my brother's shoes still lay, untouched. We had already braced ourselves for the worst. He was announced dead on the spot. His small body lay motionless, the silence heavier than the smell of burnt rubber that lingered in the air.

And then, in the midst of the chaos, she appeared. A woman, a stranger to us at the time, but someone I would come to know later. She wasn't a doctor, nor was she family, but she had something stronger than either—faith. Tears streamed down her face as she knelt beside my brother, her hands trembling as she reached toward him. Her voice cracked as she prayed, a raw and desperate plea to God. She begged for mercy, for a miracle, for His will to be done.

Then something happened.

The God of the universe, the same God I had cried out to in my loneliest moments, saw fit to use my brother as a living testimony. Against all odds, against every logical explanation, a pulse returned. The stillness in his chest gave way to the faintest rise and fall.

The paramedics sprang into action, disbelief flashing across their faces as they rushed to stabilize him. He was lifted onto a stretcher, his body battered and broken, and within moments, the whirring blades of the helicopter filled the sky. He was flown out for emergency care, beginning a battle that would last years.

The road to recovery was grueling. There were multiple surgeries, including one on his brain, followed by months in the hospital, where beeping monitors replaced the quiet nights we once knew. Physical therapy became his new routine, each movement a painful step toward regaining what had been stolen from him in an instant. But through it all, he remained what he had become that day—a living testimony of God's power.

I don't share this story just to tell you about a modern-day miracle, though it was one. I share it because, like my brother, we all have a story. We all carry wounds, both seen and unseen. And this collection of memories—these moments of struggle, survival, and self-discovery—this is mine.

I have four more brothers beyond the one you just read about. Their stories, like mine, are worth telling. And in time, you will hear them.

Colossians 3:12 (KJV) "Put on therefore, as the elect of God, holy and beloved, bowels of mercies, kindness, humbleness of mind, meekness, longsuffering."

Chapter 3:

BROTHER'S KEEPER

Not long after my brother's accident, my grand-parents came to a realization. Our living situation was far from ideal. Who could have guessed that placing a single-wide mobile home inches from a road, with five wild boys under the age of fourteen, wasn't the best idea?

That decision led us to a new chapter in our lives, one that took us to a place called Saltwell, just off Highway 645 in Inez, Kentucky. The property was tucked up in the holler, a quiet stretch of land that felt like an entirely different world compared to where we had been. This was where we relocated our single-wide, the same home that had seen so much chaos, heartbreak, and survival.

But change was coming.

My grandparents, in an unexpected and bold move, decided to take on a thirty-year mortgage. When they told us about the purchase, I couldn't wrap my head around it. Thirty years? That was longer than I had been alive. But what really mattered to me was the house itself. To my young eyes, it was huge.

We had upgraded.

A 2007 double-wide, complete with three bedrooms, two bathrooms, and a den, stood before us like a mansion. It wasn't the sprawling homes I had seen on TV, but compared to what we were used to, it might as well have been. There was space, more than we had ever known, though still not enough to avoid the ever-present reality of living with a big family. The house was meant for seven of us, but that number didn't account for the uncles who came and went, drifting in and out of our lives like restless ghosts.

This house, this place, was supposed to be a fresh start. A chance for life to settle into something steadier, something better. But life, as I was beginning to learn, never moved in a straight line. It twisted and turned, sometimes leading us to places we never expected, forcing us to grow in ways we never wanted.

Saltwell was just another stop on the journey. And life, whether we were ready or not, went on.

Not long after we settled into our new home, my mother had another baby, another boy she wasn't prepared to care for. Mamaw, with a heart as big as the sky, didn't hesitate. When he was about six months old, he came to live with us.

I still remember the day my grandparents brought him home. It was a defining moment, one that would shape the years ahead in ways none of us could have imagined. The funniest part of it all was my grandfather's firm stance before they left to visit my mother and the baby. He had repeatedly told mamaw that they were not bringing the baby back with them. It reminded me of people who take their wives to visit an animal shelter, swearing they're just looking. And yet, by the end of that day, our home had gone from a household of seven to a house of eight.

From the moment he arrived, I felt something shift. This wasn't just my younger brother. He quickly became like a son to me. There were countless nights when I was in junior high that I stayed up with mamaw, helping to feed and entertain him. I taught him to walk, changed his diapers, and made him laugh until I gave him hiccups.

Some nights, long before the sun even thought about rising, his cries would echo from the living room, keeping my exhausted mamaw awake. Even at thirteen, I felt responsible. I would quietly slide out of bed, careful not to wake my eleven-year-old brother, and tiptoe to the living room. No one asked me to, but I did it anyway. Mamaw needed a break. And deep down, I knew that if I could do anything to make things easier, I would.

As I fed or played with my little brother, Mamaw would often drift off to sleep on the couch, completely exhausted. I would gently remove her glasses, tuck a blanket around her, and continue caring for him so she could regain her strength. Sometimes, he would get too loud, his little squeals and babbles waking her up, and she would tell me to go back to bed so I could focus in class the next day. But I never minded. It was funny how I had never had a father figure myself, yet God led me to be one for my brother.

Those moments meant everything to me. I'll always cherish memories like those, especially the day I walked him through the Gospel. It was a small moment, just the two of us, but it felt big—like something that would stay with us both forever.

I've always believed that growing up without a father leaves you with two choices. You either run to God to fill that space, or you run away, searching for fulfillment in the things of this world. My brothers and I each made our choice. My oldest brother, the one who always tucked his polo shirts into his jeans, chose alcohol. That addiction spiraled into drugs, and eventually, it took his life in 2023 at just thirty-four years old.

For my next older brother, it was whatever he could get his hands on to numb the pain of feeling unloved and unwanted. He and I eventually shared a bedroom that was more like an apartment, detached from the rest of the house. We would go into the house for meals, showers, and when we needed to go number two. Beyond that, we tried not to go inside and be exposed to the madness. There were countless nights I watched him light up a homemade pop-can bong, inhaling just enough to quiet whatever storm raged inside him. If it wasn't that, it was beer—can after can, bottle after bottle—trying to drown out a lifetime of hurt. I watched him, and I wondered if he ever found what he was looking for.

I was always my older brother's keeper, making sure he got home safe no matter what situation he was in. I remember one night when he and a group of our friends were heading over to play football at someone's house. At some point, someone pulled out a handful of pills, and before I knew it, they were chewing them up like Tic Tacs.

I should have walked away. I wanted to. But fear is a powerful thing. Fear of not belonging. Fear of being abandoned. So when my brother offered me one, I took it. To this day, I have no idea what it was. Thankfully, that was the only time I joined in—unless you count the countless contact highs from babysitting him.

One night stands out among the rest. My brother had smoked some synthetic marijuana, and it hit him harder than anything I had seen before. His legs gave out beneath him, his body slumping like a puppet with its strings cut. He couldn't walk, couldn't even keep himself upright. His eyes rolled back, and for a terrifying moment, I thought I might lose him right there.

I was sixteen. He was twenty. There was no one else around to help. No one to take over when my arms started shaking. No one to call...who would actually show up. It was just me, my brother, and the long stretch of terrain between where we were and where we needed to be.

I hooked my arms under his and heaved him up, his weight pressing down on me like a sack filled with bricks. He mumbled something I couldn't understand, his head lolling forward as I adjusted my grip. Every step was a battle. The dirt and gravel beneath my feet felt unsteady, shifting as I struggled to keep us both upright. My lungs burned. My back screamed. My legs threatened to give out, but I kept going. I didn't have a choice.

The night was still, but my mind was loud. I kept thinking about all the times he should have carried me when we were kids. Not in the literal sense, but in the way older brothers are supposed to. The way they teach you things, look out for you, make you feel safe. Instead, here I was, carrying him. Not just his body, but the weight of everything that had led us to this moment.

Half a mile had never felt so long. By the time I reached our bedroom, my arms were numb. I barely had the strength to lower him onto my bed before he turned to the side and threw up everywhere. I should have been disgusted, but all I felt was relief. He was breathing. He was alive. And for that night, at least, he was home.

I made sure he was on his side so he wouldn't choke, then left him there. I guess you could say I never really had a positive role model to follow…just plenty of examples of what not to do.

Eventually, my grandfather would have enough. He'd yell for my older brothers to, "…either get the hell out of his house or he'd kick their [butts] himself." Most times, that just meant they'd crash at a neighbor's house or stay with a family member for the night. It was always temporary. My grandfather would come to his senses, realize he'd lose the check he got for raising us, and suddenly decide we were "missing." He'd call the police, reporting that we had run away from home.

Every time, the same thing happened. The police would bring my brother back, he'd get a lecture about how foolish it was to run away from such a "loving" household, and that would be the end of it. A never-ending cycle.

As you can imagine, it was only a matter of time before it was my turn.

Psalm 68:5 (KJV) "A father of the fatherless, and a judge of the widows, is God in his holy habitation."

Chapter 4:

POVERTY PAINS

Looking back, certain memories stand out like signposts, marking the circumstances we lived through. These moments, small and seemingly insignificant at the time, were reflections of a larger reality, one I didn't fully understand until much later.

Take my teeth, for example. Cavities were as much a part of me as my own skin. I never questioned why they were always there; I assumed it was just the way things were. After all, most people in my family didn't have teeth past their late twenties. It wasn't until years later that I learned brushing your teeth was something you were supposed to do every day, even when school was out for the summer. To me, brushing was more of a social courtesy—a way to keep your breath fresh when you were around other people. Even during the school year, no one in my family pushed the idea that it should be done more than once a day. Oral hygiene was never a priority; survival was.

Then there was the smoke. Thick, inescapable, always present. On any given day, five to seven people would go through one to two packs of cigarettes each, filling our small mobile home with a permanent haze. The air hung heavy with it, coating the walls, our clothes, and even our skin. There was no running from it, not in the single-wide trailer where we lived. When we finally "upgraded" to a double-wide, I was hopeful. More space meant more breathing room, a chance to escape the suffocating cloud that clung to everything. We had a little more space for the twelve or so people that usually took residence there, which made it feel less cramped, but fresh air was still a luxury.

For a brief, glorious moment, we had a smoking ban inside the new place. I was thrilled. Finally, clean air. But hope has a way of slipping through your fingers when you're not holding on tight enough. Within a few months, the rule crumbled under habit and addiction, and soon, the walls of our new home turned the same sickly yellow as the old one.

As I got older and became more interested in girls, I started paying attention to things I hadn't before—like the way I smelled. It didn't matter how much deodorant I used or how many showers I took; the cigarette smoke followed me like a shadow. My brothers and I shared a single deodorant stick and the same razors, but that wasn't the real problem. The real struggle was trying to mask the ever-present stench of cigarettes that clung to my clothes, making it impossible to blend in at school.

I grew up in a time when smoking wasn't just uncool—it was frowned upon. Only the poor Gothic kids huddled behind the school smoking cigarettes, their rebellion laced with nicotine and misplaced defiance. I wasn't one of them, but you wouldn't know that from the way I smelled. The girls I dated would wrinkle their noses and ask, *"Do you smoke?"* I'd shake my head, embarrassed, but I knew the truth was hanging in the air between us.

Eventually, I found a solution, a small, almost ridiculous trick, but it worked. Every morning, before school, I'd throw my clothes in the dryer with a few scented dryer sheets. The heat would bake in the fresh scent, masking the smoke just enough to get me through the day. It wasn't perfect, but as long as no one got too close, I could almost pretend I smelled like a normal kid. Occasionally, I would leave an extra item of clothing for the next day in the dryer and my grandparents would welcome me home with yelling for raising the electric bill by using the dryer on a single item of clothing. How foolish of me, right? They couldn't even begin to understand. Afterall, smoking was the family tradition.

I always had allergy problems, but I never realized my suffering wasn't normal until I left. A sore, swollen throat, a constant runny nose, irritated, watery eyes— these symptoms followed me like a shadow. I thought that was just how life was. Turns out, I'm allergic to cigarette smoke.

For years, I teased my now-wife about her need for allergy medication, laughing at how she depended on it. That is, until one day, she pointed out that I had the exact same symptoms. She suggested I try her over-the-counter allergy medicine. I didn't think much of it, but I took one anyway. That small decision changed my life. For the first time, I could breathe. It was as if a weight I hadn't even realized I was carrying had been lifted off my chest. I had spent my entire childhood suffocating, and I never even knew it.

That was just one of the many health struggles I endured without understanding why. Another was the way injuries were treated—or rather, ignored. I distinctly remember the time I sliced my thumb to the bone with a kitchen knife, while trying to make breakfast. Blood pooled in my palm, but before I could even process what had happened, my grandfather waved it off. He reached for a roll of black electrical tape and handed it to me like it was the cure for all wounds.

"It's fine. Ain't no need to go to the doctor," he said.

I stared at him, unsure if he was joking. He wasn't. If it hadn't been for mamaw, who insisted another family member take me to get stitches, I might have just wrapped my thumb in tape and called it a day. That was the way things were. You didn't go to the doctor unless you were dying.

And sometimes, even then, you had to wait.

I was eight years old when my appendix started to rupture. At first, we thought it was just terrible gas pains. My stomach twisted in agony, but my grandfather wasn't interested in my complaints. When I told mamaw I couldn't go to school, he grew frustrated. I loved school. It was my escape. The last thing I ever wanted was to stay home. But this pain was different. It was sharp, relentless, like something inside me was trying to tear its way out.

Annoyed by my cries, my grandfather decided he needed a break from it all. He left the house, disappearing into the hills of our holler to go herbing. It was his way of escaping. Unfortunately for me, he was also the only person in our house with a driver's license.

We lived about an hour from the nearest hospital. To make matters worse, our road was nothing but dirt and gravel—Meathouse was tucked so far away from civilization that the blacktop hadn't yet reached us. Every bump and pothole had been carved deeper by the constant rumble of coal trucks. It was the kind of road that rattled your bones on a good day. On a bad day, when your appendix was on the verge of bursting, every jolt sent fresh waves of pain through your body.

Eventually, a cousin stopped by and offered to take us to the hospital. The ride was torture. Each loose rock, each pothole, felt like a knife twisting inside me. But somehow, I made it in time. My appendix was removed, and I survived.

These are just a few of the health struggles that come with poverty. The things we endured weren't extraordinary where I came from—they were normal. But normal doesn't always mean right.

Opportunity Deserts

For my undergraduate degree, I wrote my senior seminar paper on food deserts in Appalachia, specifically in the more remote and rural parts of the region. My thesis centered on the idea that, yes, Appalachia struggles with access to affordable, quality food. However, food is far from the only resource that Appalachia lacks.

This chapter explores the broader concept of opportunity deserts in Appalachia, areas where access to essential resources such as jobs, education, healthcare, and childcare is severely limited. While these issues exist across the world, research has shown that they are particularly concentrated and persistent in Appalachia. As the Appalachian Regional Commission (ARC) reported, "The household poverty rate is 17.2 percent in the Appalachian Region, a figure slightly higher than the national rate of 15.6 percent."[3]

Despite the best intentions, many organizations, whether businesses, nonprofits, or churches, operate in silos, unwilling to collaborate toward a common goal. This fragmentation suffocates opportunities for young leaders who are eager to break the cycle of generational poverty.

Poverty, in itself, is a paradox. In some ways, our system has made it easier to remain poor than to escape it. The cycle of poverty is not just about lacking money. It is about the barriers that make climbing out feel nearly impossible. Some of these barriers are circumstantial, like a lack of education or job opportunities. Others are systemic, woven into policies that were meant to help but, in reality, keep people stuck.

A clear example of this is the benefits cliff, a term used to describe the point at which an individual earns just enough income to lose their government assistance but not enough to achieve financial stability. According to the Federal Reserve Bank of Atlanta, "Due to the gradual or sudden loss of these programs, career advancement may result in a family being financially worse off (a benefits cliff) or no better off (a benefits plateau) than before the wage increase."[4]

Think about that. A person works hard, gets a raise, and instead of moving forward, they fall backward.

Suddenly, they no longer qualify for food stamps, housing assistance, or Medicaid. Their paycheck has increased, but so have their expenses, and now they are left scrambling to cover costs that were once subsidized. In many cases, the new income is not enough to make up the difference, leaving them in a worse financial position than before.

Given this reality, why would someone take a low-paying job when it could mean losing access to essential resources? Why risk a promotion if it means being unable to afford rent or healthcare? This is not laziness. This is not a lack of ambition. This is a rational response to an irrational system. And this conundrum is not just a personal problem. It fuels the employment crisis in Appalachia and beyond, trapping entire communities in a cycle where work does not always lead to progress.

Another significant obstacle for low-income individuals is the lack of affordable and accessible childcare. For many families, especially single parents, the cost of daycare is so high that working full-time barely covers the expense. Imagine being offered a job that pays fifteen dollars an hour, only to realize that childcare alone will eat up most of your paycheck. It is an impossible equation. Without reliable, affordable childcare, many parents, especially mothers, are forced to choose between employment and caregiving. It is a choice that no one should have to make in a society that claims to value work and family.

So what is the solution? More access to good-paying jobs that take real-life circumstances into account. A good job is not just about a paycheck. It is about stability. It is about a wage that allows a person to cover their basic needs without fear. It is about employers recognizing that their workers are also parents, caregivers, and people with responsibilities outside of the workplace.

A good job is great medicine. This sentiment, echoed by economists and public health experts alike, speaks to the transformative power of stable employment. Jobs that pay fair wages, provide flexible work hours, and consider the childcare needs of their employees do not just strengthen a workforce. They actively break the cycle of poverty.

So if you are in a position to employ others, be the kind of employer who lifts people up. Offer fair wages.

Be flexible where you can. Understand that stability is what allows people to build better lives. Because sometimes, a job is not just a job. It is a bridge out of an opportunity desert. And for someone trapped in the cycle of poverty, that bridge can mean everything.

Personal Deserts

I was sixteen the first time I received a proper barber's haircut. It only happened because I had finally saved up enough money—not just for the cut itself, but also for a family member to drive me there. Gas prices had always been outrageous, and in our house, even a short trip needed careful financial consideration.

What a phenomenon it was, stepping into that shop, where the hum of clippers blended with the low chatter of men discussing everything from sports to the price of groceries. The air conditioning was a luxury I hadn't realized I'd been missing.

For the first time, I had a choice in how my hair would be cut. It was strange, almost foreign, to be asked what I wanted. Before that, haircuts had been purely functional—an act of necessity rather than preference.

Every few months, when my hair grew too long to manage, it would simply be shaved off.

Mamaw wouldn't dare cut our hair inside the house and get hair all over her floor, oh no. She had a system. She waited for a clear sky, with the sun overhead, so she could see well enough to avoid nicking us with the clippers. To make matters slightly worse, she would have us cut a hole in the bottom of a large trash bag and pop our heads through it to act as a barber cape. You can imagine just how uncomfortable this was in the boiling sun. But, in reality, our haircuts weren't dictated by time or length—they were dictated by lice. That was the real reason our hair got shaved. It was an unspoken cycle: the itching would start, the inevitable discovery would follow, and then, out came the clippers.

It wasn't just our heads that suffered. Flea bites covered our arms and legs, a constant irritation we grew used to, thanks to the dogs we always seemed to have. Our grandparents, despite struggling to afford medicine for themselves, kept those dogs around. Maybe they needed companionship, something warm and familiar that wouldn't talk back like us boys did. But without flea treatments, the dogs contributed to the never-ending problem—our home was as much theirs as it was ours, and the bugs thrived just the same.

Then, there were the grade school field trips. For most kids, these trips were a reward, a break from the monotony of schoolwork for those who would do well on a particular test or assignment. For me, they were something else entirely. The moment a trip was announced, the dread set in. The ticket was only six dollars—not much, not really—but it might as well have been six thousand. Schools often covered costs for students in need, but that required asking for help. And what kid wants to do that? Who wants to be singled out and pitied?

So, about a week before the trip, I'd start asking for the money. It would usually go something like this...

"Hey, Gramps! I've been doing well in school."

A long drag from his cigarette. "Yeah, that's good."

I tried to keep my tone casual, not too eager. "I think the school is going to take us on a trip as a reward."

Silence.

"Maybe even to watch one of those new 3D movies."

Another drag. "That'll be pretty expensive for them to take all you kids to the movies."

"Well, about that... They've agreed to cover part of the cost, but we still have to pay just $6."

"Well, that's not much of a reward if you still have to pay. I guess you'll be staying at school that day then."

My heart sank, but I pushed forward. "Are you sure you can't come up with the money for me to go?"

He exhaled, his voice sharpening. "Yeah, if you kids would quit taking so many showers and eating so much, maybe I could. The electric bill was X amount last month, and the water bill was X amount. You're gonna burn up the washer, dryer, stove, and hot water tank doing that."

A final drag. "Ain't no need for you to be going anywhere anyhow."

That was it.

That was the phrase that ruled our house. "Ain't no need..." It had consumed him. At some point, the struggle had taken over everything—every thought, every action. If I pressed any harder, he would start to yell. Then mamaw would step in to defend me, which would only make him yell louder. The cursing would follow, echoing through the house, filling the air like the smoke from his cigarette.

Most nights, I'd end up in bed with tears in my eyes, staring at the ceiling, wondering why I even bothered. What was the point of doing well in school? What was the reward for trying?

But sometimes, just sometimes, when I got up in the middle of the night for a drink of water, I'd find six dollars' worth of coins laid out on the kitchen counter. Having waited until my grandfather went to bed, mamaw had scrunched them together—her quiet way of telling me she believed in me, even if the world didn't.

I was invited to join the academic team at a very young age. The excitement was immediate, but so was the fear. I wanted so badly to say yes, to be around my peers more, to feel like I belonged. More than anything, I wanted an extracurricular activity—any reason to stay after school, any excuse to be away from home for a little longer. But I already knew the answer. My grandparents wouldn't allow it. Staying after school meant needing a ride home, and that meant gas money, something we never had enough of.

I never brought anyone to our house. The fear of someone realizing we were poor was overwhelming. What if they saw the single-wide trailer? Or later, our so-called mansion of a double-wide? What if they noticed how different our family was? What if they witnessed my grandfather's temper?

School clothes were possibly the worst. Every year, just before school started, we got one, maybe two, outfits from Walmart. That was all. And yet, I was grateful for the Family Resource Center programs at school. They assigned me a sponsor, someone who, though a stranger, cared enough to provide what we couldn't. They bought clothes, shoes, gift cards, and, best of all, they wrote letters. Encouraging words that made me feel seen. My sponsor stayed with me through most of my school years, and I always wrote thank-you cards in return.

The school tried to be discreet. They never made a show of it, never labeled me as the poor kid. But I still lived in constant fear that people knew, that they saw. So, I learned how to keep up the façade. I answered everyday questions carefully.

"What did you get for Christmas?"

"My brothers and I got a basketball goal."

That was always the way, one shared gift for all of us. Not because we wanted to share, but because it was all we could have. And yet, when I answered, I made it sound like there was more. Like Christmas had been full. Like we had enough...I feel the need to add here that material gifts are not what Christmas is all about. To be clear, the only reason we exchange gifts should be to emphasize the ultimate gift offered to us from God in the form of his son Jesus coming to this earth to be offered as a gift of repentance for our sins. With that being said, many families get so busy and caught up with the commercialism of the holiday season that youth are often not taught the true meaning and therefore end up subscribing to the materialistic pressure that society places on this joyous season...

Because admitting otherwise was never an option.

Dating was particularly difficult. I built up barriers on purpose, holding back the truth about my parents not being the ones raising me for as long as I could. I didn't want to explain why. I didn't want to scare anyone off. The thought always crossed my mind—I'm not like them.

I never had money for dates. I never even had a ride to free outings. I distinctly remember breaking up with girls before summer break because I knew I wouldn't be able to afford movie dates. It wasn't just the cost of the ticket. I didn't have gas money to get there. I wasn't allowed to go to the pool because of the $2 fee. Sometimes, I even ended things before a girl's birthday because I knew I couldn't afford to get her anything.

Sports were never an option for me either. Gas money was always the issue. I only got to play in a condensed basketball league once, thanks to an uncle who volunteered to take me to games in fifth grade. Then again, in eighth grade, when a cousin agreed to drive me. The funny thing about that cousin—he was always around because he had just been released from prison for stabbing his father five years earlier. He needed a place to stay, and of course, my grandparents took him in. The sad part? I wasn't just excelling in the classroom. I had real potential on the basketball court too.

Basketball was my outlet. That goal we got one Christmas became my everything. Rain, snow, sleet, or hail, I was out there on the dirt court, releasing my built-up anger, stress, fear, and depression. That was where, as a young man, God would speak to me. It was in those quiet moments that He gave me encouragement, reminding me that I had a purpose. That I mattered. That I was loved, even when I didn't feel it.

That dirt court became my escape from the madness that always waited for me inside our house. The second we stepped through the door, we were met with complaints, yelling, something we had done wrong. Some days, I would come home from school, throw my backpack inside the back door, and stay outside shooting until I could no longer see the rim. Some nights, we stayed longer, guessing where the hoop was in the dark.

I share this with you to remind you; *never to judge a book by its cover.* Some children are simply victims of their surroundings. There very well may be a good reason why they're falling asleep in your class or sluggish at practice. Offer them a little grace.

Limiting Factors

Gay Hendricks[5] talks about the "upper limit" as the amount of positive feeling you allow yourself to experience before unconsciously sabotaging it. Brianna Wiest builds on this idea in The Mountain Is You, explaining how self-sabotage isn't always obvious. It often disguises itself as rational decision-making. It feels like logic, like being responsible, like making the right choice. But in reality, it's just our subconscious pulling us back into what feels safe and familiar, even when that familiarity is a struggle.

I can't count the number of times I've done this to myself. If you remember, I mentioned sabotaging in reference to my workout gloves. That was a small example, but the truth is, it's uncomfortable to step beyond what you know. It's uncomfortable to put yourself out there, to risk failure, to be seen in a new way. But that discomfort is exactly where growth happens.

I have a perfect example.

After transitioning careers, I received a substantial check from a forced savings account I had built over three and a half years at my previous job. That kind of money in my bank account felt unreal. At the time, I was only a few years removed from college, still adjusting to the idea that I wasn't financially poor anymore. I had spent so many years living month to month as a child and paycheck to paycheck after beginning to earn my own wage, scraping by, convincing myself that I just needed one big break to feel secure. Then the break came, and instead of using it wisely, I let my subconscious pull me right back into the cycle I knew best.

So, what did I do with the money?

I bought a Mustang. Not a practical family car. Not an investment. A Mustang. And I had a newborn at the time.

I told myself I deserved it and that it was my reward for working hard. That I would still be fine financially because I had a steady job and could make it work. It all made sense in my head. And then, just a few months later, it didn't.

That car didn't last long. I convinced myself I needed something else. Something better. Something that fit me more. So I traded it in for a Jeep Wrangler. Another impractical choice. Another financial mistake. But at the time, I didn't see it that way. I believed I was just making decisions that suited my lifestyle. I wasn't sabotaging myself—I was just upgrading.

Eventually, I came to my senses and downgraded to a 7,000 dollar F-150. That should have been the end of it. That should have been the moment I learned my lesson and made a smarter financial choice.

But no.

A few months later, I started getting that restless feeling again. I started convincing myself I needed something newer. Something nicer. Something that made me feel successful. So I sold the F-150, put the money down on a much newer truck, and within months, reality hit.

I couldn't actually afford the payments.

I had to sell it at a loss, effectively setting my 7,000 dollars on fire.

And that's the tricky part about self-sabotage. It doesn't announce itself. It doesn't come with flashing red lights or a warning label. It creeps in quietly, whispering in your ear that this one decision won't hurt. That you've worked hard and deserve this. That it's not a big deal.

And if you're not careful, you wake up one day and realize you've walked yourself right back into the very thing you were trying to escape.

There were so many smarter things I could have done with that money. I did none of them. That mistake still stings, but it also drives me to be wiser.

So if you see someone talking themself into something that deep down, they know isn't the best move, help them pause. Take a breath. Be brutally honest with themself, and ask, is this growth? Or is this just another way of keeping yourself exactly where you've always been?

Isaiah 61:7 (KJV) "For your shame ye shall have double; and for confusion they shall rejoice in their portion: therefore in their land they shall possess the double: everlasting joy shall be unto them."

Chapter 5:

THE NIGHT I LEFT

For years, I waited by the phone on my birthday, hoping and praying that my parents would call. I didn't expect gifts or grand gestures. I wasn't even asking them to show up physically. I just wanted to hear their voices, to have them acknowledge that, on this day years ago, I came into the world and mattered to them. But those calls never rang.

We didn't celebrate birthdays in our house. There was never a cake, never candles, never a song. The reason was as predictable as it was painful. Money. The idea of setting aside a few dollars for something as simple as a birthday was considered a luxury, and luxuries weren't for people like us. I will say at sixteen; I was mocked by my family for asking to get my driver's permit and a car by them getting me a little cake from the local grocery with a toy car on top, certainly what every aspiring young man wants for his sixteenth birthday.

By the time I turned seventeen, I didn't care about a party. I didn't care about presents or surprises. I only wanted one thing, something small, something that most teenagers took for granted. I wanted my driver's permit. Not because I had dreams of speeding down our curvy Appalachian roads with my windows down, blasting music, and feeling free. My reasons were far more serious. I just wanted one normal teenage experience. I wanted a way out. A job. A car. A future.

Mamaw, always the thoughtful one, asked what I wanted that year. I told her the same thing I had told her the year before: my driver's permit. That was it. Just a chance to take a step toward something better. But she made the mistake of asking me in front of my grandfather.

His response was immediate, sharp, and dismissive.

"Ain't no need for that."

I felt my body tense, but I kept my voice steady. "What do you mean?"

"Because I said so," he shot back, his tone leaving no room for argument.

That was the problem. His mind was a closed door, locked and rusted shut. The thought of me wanting to grow, to take control of my life, was foreign to him. He never thought beyond the present moment, beyond how every decision impacted him financially. He wasn't thinking about my future. He was thinking about his wallet.

I pushed back, trying to reason with him, but reason had no place in that house. The conversation quickly turned to yelling, and like a rebellious child, I was sent to my room for daring to want more.

Later, I learned the real reason for his refusal. If I got a job, he would lose the government check he received for raising me. And when I finally confronted him about it, the conversation exploded into an argument I would never forget.

"Yeah, you can walk to a job after school each day," he sneered. "As long as you pay me the $300 a month I'd lose."

I stared at him, stunned. He was serious.

I did the math in my head, what I'd make at a minimum-wage job, how much would be left after giving him his cut, and what little I'd have to save for the things I actually needed. The numbers didn't add up. They never would.

It was never about me growing up. It was never about my independence. It was about control.

The idea that I wanted to finish high school, work a job, and build a life for myself was unthinkable to him. He saw no future, no possibilities beyond the four walls of that house. But I did.

And that's what made me different.

Roughly a week after my seventeenth birthday, Mamaw looked at me with a soft but knowing expression and asked, "Are you ready to go?"

I frowned. "Go where?"

"To the courthouse to take your driver's permit test," she said, like it was the most obvious thing in the world. This was particularly funny due to the fact that even after all her years, she never became a licensed driver herself.

For a moment, I just stared at her, unsure if I had heard correctly. My heart started pounding. This was it. My one shot. If I failed, I knew there wouldn't be a second chance. My grandfather would make sure of that. There would be no redo, no trip back to the courthouse, no encouragement to try again.

I whispered a quick prayer, asking God to help me remember everything I had studied, then bolted for the car before anything could change. I had studied the manuals like my life depended on it just in case some soul would take me to the local courthouse for testing. Thankfully, Mamaw had paid someone in our family to take us.

The moment I saw the word *PASSED* on the screen, I nearly collapsed in relief. I had done it. I had actually done it. Mamaw smiled, her eyes shining with quiet pride, and reached into her purse. I watched as she handed over the last of her "allowance" to pay for that little piece of plastic that meant everything to me.

That's the kind of heart she has. Even now.

When we got home, she told my grandfather what she had done. He barely reacted. Just a slow, stiff nod, his jaw tightening ever so slightly. But I knew that simple gesture carried more weight than it seemed. I was sure that behind closed doors, there would be an argument. A quiet war waged between mamaw's kindness and my grandfather's need for control.

It wasn't long before I started paying for that war.

Suddenly, everything I did seemed to irritate him. The way I walked, the way I spoke, even the way I breathed in his presence. The yelling became constant. The tension in the house thickened like a storm rolling in, and I knew it was only a matter of time before the thunder struck.

That night, it finally did.

It was a Wednesday, like any other. I had gone to church, just like I did every week. When I stepped through the front door, I barely had time to take a breath before my grandfather's voice rang out.

"There he is!"

I froze. His tone was sharp, charged with something I couldn't quite place yet.

The yelling started immediately. Words flying like arrows. Accusations I couldn't even process fast enough. I stood there, caught in the storm, waiting for a break in the chaos. Eventually, he barked out the question he had been holding back.

"Where have you been?"

I blinked. "At church. Like every Wednesday."

Mamaw, her voice thick with frustration, cut in. "I've been trying to tell him that for the last two hours, but he won't listen."

She looked exhausted. Her hands trembled slightly as she tried to reason with him, but it was no use. He was too far gone, his anger fueled by something deeper than just my absence. Mamaw's act of defiance by helping me get my driver's permit was finally coming to head. He kept yelling, kept cursing, kept threatening.

I didn't say a word. Instead, I sat beside Mamaw, trying to ease her nerves, letting my presence tell her that she wasn't alone in this. She would often stay in the living room watching *her shows* while he would remain in the den.

But then she snapped.

"Would you just leave him alone already?!" she shouted, her voice cutting through the air like a whip.

The room went still.

My grandfather turned toward her slowly, his eyes dark and cold. And then, in a voice that sent ice down my spine, he said, "You better shut up unless you want to get your mouth smacked."

Everything inside me revolted.

For years, I had taken his cruelty. I had swallowed every insult, endured every threat, and absorbed every ounce of his rage without fighting back. But this? No. Not her. Not the one person who had truly cared about me my whole life.

I shot to my feet before I even realized what I was doing. My voice came out low and steady, but there was no mistaking the steel behind it.

"You hurt her, and it'll be the last thing you do."

The air in the room shifted. His face twisted a mixture of shock and fury. In all my years, I had never challenged him like this. This was not the first time one of their arguments escalated to physical threats, but this time was different.

"Shut up," he spat. "Get outside to your room."

I didn't move.

"I said get out!"

Still, I didn't move.

I had no intention of leaving Mamaw alone with him, not in this state. And when he realized I wasn't backing down, I heard it. The sound of heavy, furious footsteps charging toward me.

"Mr. Tough Guy," he growled.

Before I could react, his hand flew through the air and struck me in the face.

I had experienced occasional physical discipline of correction over the years, but this was different.

I had spent years enduring his words, his intimidation, his control. But never this. I had watched my older brothers take the hits. I had heard the stories and seen the aftermath, but until now, I had been spared. Tonight, that changed.

Pain exploded across my face as my jaw began to swell, but something else surged through me, something hotter and sharper than the sting of being hit in the face.

My open hand curled into a fist.

My vision blurred. Not from the pain, but from something far worse. Betrayal.

I had spent my whole life knowing what kind of man he was, but somehow, some small part of me had still believed I was safe. No matter how cruel his words were, no matter how much he controlled every aspect of my life, he wouldn't cross that line. But he had.

In case you were wondering, no, I didn't hit him back. I wanted to. God, I wanted to more than I wanted to take my next breath. Every muscle in my body tensed, my fists clenched so tightly that my nails bit into my palms. But I didn't do it. Not because I was scared. Not because I respected him. But because of her.

Mamaw's voice broke through the chaos, shaking with desperation.

"Please," she begged, "please don't hurt him. Just leave."

At first, I thought Mamaw was pleading with him to stop, to leave me alone. But then I realized she was talking to me, telling me not to hurt him.

I tore my eyes away from the sad excuse of a man in front of me, from the smug, taunting look that dared me to swing. I wanted to wipe that expression off his face, make him feel even a fraction of the rage burning through me. But I wouldn't. I wouldn't give him the satisfaction.

Instead, I turned around and walked away.

I spent that night pacing the mile-long stretch of our one-lane road, walking up and down in the pitch black, my breath coming out in sharp, uneven bursts. I had nowhere to go. Nowhere that felt safe. Each car's headlights that passed by would reflect off the tears of anger flowing down my face.

I had tried knocking on my friend's window next door. I would often use a long stick to knock on his second floor window when things would get out of hand at home. Little did he know, I was desperate for a place to crash for the night, but there was no answer. So I just walked. For hours, I wandered in the dark, looking up at the night sky and pleading with God.

"Why me? Why do I have to live this life when other kids have real parents who love them? Why was I born into this?"

I got no answer. Just the sound of my footsteps on the pavement, the distant hum of crickets, and the weight of my own thoughts pressing down on me.

By two in the morning, I was exhausted. I decided to try my friend's window one more time. This time, he finally stirred, groggily rubbing his eyes before realizing who was standing outside in the cold. Without hesitation, he let me in. We often kept a long 2x6 board that I would use to scale my way into the window. He holding onto one end while I dug the other into the ground below. That was until it broke one night, so we settled for the front door this time.

That night, I slept in a place that wasn't my home, yet somehow, I felt safer there than I ever had in my own bed.

The next morning, I woke up at a decent time, took a quick shower, borrowed some clothes, and rode with my friend to school. I walked through those hallways pretending nothing had happened. Pretending my home life hadn't just imploded. Pretending I wasn't spending the entire day wondering where I was going to sleep that night.

Then, during class, my teacher called me to the front.

"You've got a phone call."

All eyes were on me as I stood up. I could feel the weight of their stares and the quiet curiosity of my classmates as I made my way to the front of the room. Nobody ever called me at school. I forced my face into something neutral, something that wouldn't raise questions.

I picked up the receiver, and the familiar, gentle voice of my mamaw filled my ears while tears began to fill my eyes.

"I checked your room last night," she said softly. "You weren't there."

After the dust settled, after *he* had stomped off to bed, she had gone looking for me.

I gripped the phone tighter. My fingers felt stiff, my knuckles white. "I didn't come back," I said simply. "And I don't plan to. I'm not stepping back into that house. I'm not looking at *that man* again."

She let out a tired sigh, the kind that carried years of stress and heartbreak. "I know, sweetheart. But you have to. He's already talking about calling the sheriff and telling them to bring you back home forcefully."

A sharp pang shot through me. The classroom around me blurred for a second, but I couldn't let it show. I clenched my jaw, blinking fast, keeping my back straight. I couldn't let them see. Couldn't let them hear the rage bubbling under my skin.

I closed my eyes briefly, fury and exhaustion washing over me in equal waves. I knew exactly why he was threatening that. It wasn't about me. It was about that check. That precious few hundred dollars he got every month for raising me.

For a moment, I considered calling his bluff. Let him get the cops involved. Let them drag me back. Maybe then, someone would finally see what was happening behind closed doors. But I knew better. The system didn't work like that.

Mamaw pleaded with me, her voice breaking. "If they take you, they won't bring you back here. They'll put you in juvie." Without saying the words, we both knew he would paint the narrative of me simply being an uncontrollable, rebellious teenager.

I wanted to fight it. I wanted to tell her I didn't care. But I couldn't do that to her, not after everything she had done for me.

So I swallowed the lump in my throat, forcing my voice to stay even. "Fine," I said, as if it didn't matter.

And then I walked back to my seat like nothing had happened.

I'd like to pause here for just a moment and ask a bold question to my educators who might be reading. Would you have noticed? Would you have noticed me wiping the tears from my face just before turning to walk back to my seat? I assure you, no matter how hard I tried to act like that call didn't just happen, my mood showed it to everyone that day. Ask yourself, "How many of my students have experienced similar calls or texts, and I don't know?"

The tears on my face or the anger outbursts that day are only a couple of the telltale signs of a student struggling at home. Other signs take different forms, like poor hygiene, falling asleep in class, grades slipping, isolation, struggling with loud noises, and the list goes on. I do not even begin to pretend the weight our teachers and others who work with youth carry. Your roles are so valuable, and maybe, just maybe, you can make an even greater impact by being intentional about searching for similar clues.

That evening, I went back to my grandparents' house.

For a week, I didn't say a single word to *him*. Not one. I avoided him at all costs, walking on eggshells, slipping in and out of rooms as quietly as I could. If he told me to do something, I did it, but only because I wanted to avoid another explosion. He never apologized. I never expected him to. But some small, foolish part of me had hoped he would.

It took him exactly seven days to blow up again.

I honestly couldn't tell you what set him off this time. Maybe I made his coffee too weak. Maybe I vacuumed the living room the wrong way. Maybe I washed the dishes in a way that irritated him. It didn't matter. It never did.

Whatever it was, it sent him into a rage. And this time, I knew I couldn't stay much longer.

There was no physical abuse this time, but it didn't take a punch to the face for me to realize my time under his roof was over.

I remember kneeling down to tie my shoes, my fingers tightening with each loop, when he delivered what he thought was a prophecy.

"Yeah, that's right," he sneered. "You're never going to do anything with your life. You're going to end up just like your older brothers. You'll drop out of school, never get a job, and come crawling back, begging to stay."

I didn't respond. I didn't argue. I just pulled my laces tight, stood up, and walked out the door. He had no idea that, unlike my brothers before me, I would never come back.

The next few weeks were a blur of uncertainty. I bounced from a friend's house to an uncle's house to anywhere that had a couch and a little mercy to spare. I had left with nothing but three outfits, and every day was a battle to keep them clean for school.

I remember one night in particular. I was staying with someone who didn't have a dryer, so I washed my clothes in the sink and laid them over the only heat source in the house—a small space heater. I sat in front of it, watching the steam rise, praying both that my shirt would be dry before morning and that I wouldn't catch the house on fire. My shirt had a few burn marks and my jeans weren't even remotely dry, but I told myself that no one would notice anyway.

I never knew where I'd sleep at night, but one thing was certain. I was going to prove my grandfather wrong.

And I did.

I never set foot in my grandparents' house as a youth again. I woke up every morning and went to school, no matter where I had laid my head the night before. I had to get creative, memorizing the school bus routes as I moved from one side of the county to the other. I also had to get creative with forging my guardian's signature for bus slip permissions. If you're reading this Mamaw, sorry for you finding out this way. I hope you aren't too disappointed. I had to make it work.

Eventually, word of what happened reached one of my cousins. He called and told me I could stay with him. I hesitated at first, but my options were running out. Again, he had just been released from prison, but at the time, that didn't seem nearly as concerning as the alternative—sleeping under a bridge.

During that time, I managed to get my driver's license. I bought my first vehicle. I found a job. I got accepted into multiple colleges.

And, most importantly, my childhood best friend became so much more.

A Godsend

Shortly after moving in, something shifted. For the first time in a long time, I wasn't embarrassed by the house I was living in. It wasn't perfect, but it wasn't the kind of place that made me hesitate before inviting someone over. And because of that, my best friend since second grade, finally became a regular part of my world again.

She started coming over for cookouts, pool parties, and movie nights. It felt easy, familiar, like slipping back into a piece of my childhood I had nearly lost. But something was different now. Slowly, without me realizing it at first, God began to soften my heart.

I had spent years running. Running from my past, from my pain, from the reality of my situation. I had gone from one toxic relationship to another, searching for something that would fill the emptiness I carried everywhere I went. By the time I was eighteen, I had already faced four pregnancy scares. I was looking for happiness in all the wrong places, blindly chasing a sense of belonging that always slipped through my fingers.

And the entire time, Daisha was right there.

She had always been there. Watching. Listening. Sticking by my side through every mistake, every bad decision, every heartbreak. And I was too blind to see her.

At some point, she started looking less like the friend I had grown up with and more like the person I wanted to build a future with. But realizing that and actually doing something about it were two very different things. It took me a while to man up and ask her out. When I finally did, she didn't hesitate. She jumped headfirst into a relationship with a guy who, quite frankly, had no idea how to treat a woman the way she deserved.

That first year was rough.

Before Daisha, relationships had always been simple in my mind. They were transactional. I was with someone for what they could offer me, and when the excitement faded, I moved on. It was never something I put much thought into. It was just how things were. I didn't see anything wrong with it because no one had ever taught me otherwise. I had never seen a healthy relationship up close. Love, commitment, and sacrifice were foreign concepts to me. I thought relationships were about what you could take, not what you could build.

But that wasn't going to work with Daisha.

She was different from anyone I had ever been with. She wasn't interested in shallow connections or temporary feelings. She wasn't going to give herself away just because it was expected. She had convictions, ones that ran deep. She was determined to save herself for marriage, and she wasn't going to compromise that for me or anyone else. I had spent years moving through relationships without ever having to slow down and actually build something meaningful.

Looking back now, I am grateful for the foundation her parents built in her from a young age. At the time, though, I was clueless. I didn't know how to have a relationship that wasn't built on physical attraction. I didn't know how to connect with someone on a deeper level. I didn't know how to be patient, how to be present, or how to build trust without expecting something in return.

That first year forced me to unlearn everything I thought I knew about relationships. It forced me to look beyond the surface to understand what it meant to truly love someone, not just want them. It was uncomfortable. It challenged me in ways I wasn't ready for. But Daisha was patient. She didn't push me away when I struggled. She didn't give up on me when I got frustrated. She simply stood her ground, showing me through her actions what real love looked like.

I didn't know it then, but she was teaching me how to love the right way.

…and I wanted to try.

Daisha wasn't just another girl; she was the one person who had been with me through everything—my childhood, my worst moments, my mistakes. She had stood by me, offering advice and helping me navigate relationships, all while secretly hoping for her own chance.

I don't say that as a brag. If anything, it's the opposite. I was foolish. Stupid. Too blind to recognize what was right in front of me. If I had any sense at all, I would have loved her sooner. I would have spared her the pain of watching me fall for all the wrong people. I hope you can appreciate and learn from the embarrassment I share here. Maybe even educate other young men on the matter.

But somehow, she stuck around.

And thankfully, after everything, she still chose me.

She has put up with me for twelve years now (at the time of writing this), and I can honestly say—at least from my side and she may disagree—we are happily married.

Daisha and I had not been together long when we were forced to face a question that neither of us was quite ready for—what were we going to do with our lives after graduating high school?

The world felt wide open, full of possibilities, but the weight of choosing the right path pressed down on me. I knew I wanted to help people, to make a difference in some way, but I had no idea what that would look like. I bounced from one idea to another. At first, I wanted to be a Marine. The thought of wearing that uniform, serving my country, and proving my strength felt right. But something about it didn't stick. Then, I considered becoming a police officer, thinking maybe I could be the kind of authority figure I never had growing up. That, too, didn't feel quite like the answer I was searching for. It wasn't until I received a life-altering scholarship in my senior year that everything shifted.

Suddenly, the idea of becoming a behavioral health professional took root in my mind. It felt purposeful and meaningful. For the first time, I had a vision for my future.

Daisha had her own plans, her own dreams, and they didn't perfectly align with mine. She had her sights set on one college, while I had mine set on another. At first, we believed we could make it work. But as the reality of distance sank in, so did the doubts.

We prayed about it. We fought about it. We wrestled with what felt like an impossible choice. She wanted to pursue her education her way, and I wanted the same for myself. But we also knew that we had something worth holding onto. After many long conversations, sleepless nights, and more than a few stubborn arguments, we finally came to a decision.

Instead of going our separate ways, we chose to downgrade, or at least that's what we thought at the time, to a small school tucked away in the mountains of Knott County, Kentucky. What we didn't realize then was that this so-called downgrade would become one of the best decisions of our lives.

Alice Lloyd College wasn't just another school. It was a place built on values, and those values would change the course of our relationship. The school had strict rules—rules that, at the time, felt frustrating but would later become the very thing I was most grateful for.

Men weren't allowed in the women's dorms. Women weren't allowed in the men's. There was a curfew that kept students accountable. It wasn't about punishment or control. It was about creating an environment where we could focus on what truly mattered.

I needed that structure more than I realized.

For a few months after we graduated, Daisha had been helping me pay rent for a place while she still lived at home with her parents. We knew there was no point in waiting any longer. We wanted to honor God, honor each other, and step into the next chapter of our lives together. And so, we did. We graduated college early in the fall semester and were married that following May.

But even as I built a new life with Daisha, even as I took steps toward a future that was finally mine to shape, there was still a part of me that longed for something I should have let go of a long time ago.

Approval.

Despite everything that had happened, despite the way they treated me, I still wanted my grandparents to be proud of me. They were the only parents I had ever known, and some part of me still craved their validation.

It never came.

After I left their house at seventeen, they never once called to check on me. Not once.

I write this now, well over a decade later, and still, no messages have come. No congratulatory texts. No words of encouragement. The people who raised me, who pulled me out of child services, who once told me they loved me, never reached out to see how I was doing.

But I don't write this for pity. I don't share this to dwell on what I never received.

I share this to remind you of something far more important that you may need to share with someone.

You don't escape poverty for the people you leave behind. You don't work hard and break cycles to make them proud. You do it for yourself because you know that breaking free is the key to creating a better future, to changing your family tree. You do it for the family you will one day create, for the life you want to build, and for the legacy you want to leave.

Every step you take, every sacrifice you make, is not just about lifting others; it's about lifting yourself out of the patterns that once defined you. You don't endure struggles just for the approval of those around you. You do it because you know that your journey is about more than just escaping; it's about building a foundation for the future. The reality is that no one is going to do it for you. Furthermore, the ones closest to you will probably never understand; they certainly didn't in my scenario.

The people you'll eventually inspire, the family you'll support, and the generations who will look to you for strength will see your resilience, your dedication, and your hard-earned success. You do it for yourself, but in doing so, you pave the way for everyone who will follow.

Leviticus 25:35-38 (KJV)

35 And if thy brother be waxen poor, and fallen in decay with thee; then thou shalt relieve him: yea, though he be a stranger, or a sojourner; that he may live with thee.

36 Take thou no usury of him, or increase: but fear thy God; that thy brother may live with thee.

37 Thou shalt not give him thy money upon usury, nor lend him thy victuals for increase.

38 I am the Lord your God, which brought you forth out of the land of Egypt, to give you the land of Canaan, and to be your God.

Chapter 6:

THE COAT OF
MANY COLORS

I am not throwing away my shot.

I am not throwing away my shot.

I am just like my country, I am young, scrappy, and hungry, and I'm not throwing away my shot."–Hamilton (Broadway Musical)[6]

I made it out.

I of course do not mean the physical location. Poverty's grip goes so much deeper than mere physical location. I made it out of the situation that poverty brought about. Not many people from my hometown can say that. Not many from my family can either. The struggles that defined the generations before me do not define me. The battles my ancestors fought, the burdens they carried, are no longer mine to bear.

My son will never question whether he is loved. He will never sit in the quiet ache of an unanswered phone call on his birthday, wondering why the people who brought him into this world can't be bothered to remember. He will never have to carry the weight of absence, of uncertainty, of wondering if he was ever enough because I will be there.

My wife will never lose sleep over me. She will never wonder if I am where I said I would be, never second-guess the vows we exchanged, never wake up to the kind of betrayal that seeps through generations. She will never have to heal from me. The cycle of brokenness that lived in my bloodline ends here.

I wasn't supposed to make it this far. The odds weren't in my favor. I could have been another statistic, another story people shake their heads at but quickly forget. But I refused.

I became one of the first in my family to not only graduate high school, but also college, and graduate school. Each step defied everything the world expected of me. But I didn't get here alone.

There were people who saw a future for me when I could barely see past the next day. A high school principal who took a risk and invested in interview scenarios with me, in hopes of giving me an edge, when I had nothing to offer in return but simply untapped potential. A cousin who opened their home when I had nowhere else to go. Teachers who fought for me when I had no fight left in me. Business owners who gave me a chance when I had no experience, no resume—just a willingness to work. And Daisha. The woman who saw my past, my flaws, my broken pieces, and still chose to love me.

God pulled me out of the wreckage of my past. He shattered the chains of poverty, addiction, and dependency that had wrapped around my family for generations. But He didn't free me so that I could walk away untouched. He placed a burden in my heart—not just for my wife, not just for my son, but for the ones still stuck where I used to be.

I will never go back. I will never be what they said I would be.

I am not throwing away my shot.

Genesis 37 tells the story of Joseph. I know, I know—you've probably heard it a hundred times. But stay with me. I'm not here to talk about Joseph being his father's favorite or the coat that made his brothers burn with jealousy. I want to talk about them. The brothers.

Because that is where I relate.

I know what it's like to look at the people you grew up with and feel the weight of unspoken questions. To wonder why life took you in one direction while it carried them somewhere else. To wrestle with guilt, with frustration, with the aching desire to help but not knowing how.

I have always struggled with how to support my brothers. Not just my blood brothers but the ones who shared my struggles. The ones who walked the same cracked sidewalks, faced the same closed doors and heard the same voices telling them what they would never become. I have spent years asking myself the same question. Do I offer them a hand up or a handout? Do I give them a fish to satisfy the hunger gnawing at them today? Or do I teach them how to fish, knowing they might not have the strength to wait for a catch?

The roads we walked weren't identical, but they were close enough. We came from the same place, faced the same limits, and lived in the same opportunity deserts.

So why did we end up so different? It wasn't luck. It wasn't some random twist of fate. It was a series of choices, some small, some life-altering, that pulled me forward step by step. Choices that were painful, that required sacrifice, that meant walking away from things I once held close.

I don't have all the answers. I don't know why some of us made it out while others got stuck. But what I do know is this—I cannot let my progress make me forget the people still struggling. If I have the ability to reach back, to guide someone else toward the choices that saved me, then I have to try.

Because, unlike Joseph, I am not waiting for my brothers to come to me. I am going back for them.

We were raised under the same roof, ate from the same pot, and learned from the same hard lessons. We all knew what it meant to go without, to stretch a meal, to wear struggle like a second skin. The hands that raised us were firm, sometimes too firm, shaping us with discipline and desperation in equal measure. We grew up knowing the sharp edge of survival, the way it cuts deep and leaves no room for softness.

And yet, when we finally stepped out of that house, we each carried something different. Different wounds. Different regrets. Different paths that led us to places we never imagined.

Brother one had potential. He had a mind that could have taken him anywhere, a heart that once held dreams bigger than the neighborhood we grew up in. But addiction is a thief. It doesn't just steal in one night; it takes in pieces, slowly, patiently, until there's nothing left to fight back with.

For years, it kept him in its grip, dragging him under. It changed him. The kindness in his voice faded. The light in his eyes dimmed. He didn't treat his wife the way she deserved and didn't show up for his kids the way a father should. And when he left this world, he didn't just leave behind his name. He left behind seven children, each of them forced to navigate a life that should have been guided by his hand.

In the end, addiction didn't just take him. It reached beyond him, weaving its way into the lives he should have been there to shape. It left gaps that no amount of love, no amount of effort, could ever truly fill.

Brother two is the older brother that I carried for about half a mile on my shoulder just to have him throw up in my bed. You see, he struggled with anger more than anything. Something that he still carries with him. He was also the one who received the most physical abuse from our grandfather while growing up. He was twenty years old and trying to re-enroll in high school as a freshman. He has had his share of broken relationships; something that seems to haunt our family. However, I will say, day after day, shift after shift, he's shown up, put in the hours, and carved out a steady twelve-year career in a restaurant.

The problem was never his work ethic. The problem was everything else.

His home life was a storm with no shelter, a foundation so unstable that no amount of effort could keep the walls from shaking. He built a life on uncertain ground, trying to create stability with nothing but his own hands. But hands can only hold so much before they give out.

He could have gotten out. Maybe he still can. But how do you break free when every step forward is met with something pulling you back?

Brother three could have healed—at least physically. The accident shattered him, but not beyond repair. His body had the potential to recover, to regain the strength that had been stolen from him. But healing isn't just about time. It's about effort, about pushing through pain even when every muscle screams for relief.

And he needed help. The kind of help that demands patience, persistence, and someone standing beside you saying, "Keep going," even when you want to stop.

Our grandparents had already given all they had. They had spent too many years raising too many children, their nerves worn thin long before we ever came along. They didn't have it in them to push him, to insist that he fight for his recovery. So when he said, "It hurts," they let him stop.

And that was it. His body never fully recovered. The strength that could have come back never did.

But the physical scars were only part of it.

Because once you stop believing you can heal, the real damage begins.

Mentally, he never moved far past that moment his life was forever changed. However, he graduated high school a couple years before me. He may have needed a little extra assistance, but he still earned his diploma.

However, it's as if time froze when he was eight years old, trapping his mind in that space even as his body continued to grow. He gets around with a walker, but he falls often. The people around him either laugh when he stumbles or scold him for not being careful. No one stops to help him stand. No one encourages him to try again. He could have gotten out. But how can you escape something when the people closest to you don't believe you ever will?

Brother four is me.

The one and only to prioritize education.

I was first to believe that life could be different, that something more was waiting beyond the small, broken world we grew up in.

I got engaged to my childhood best friend, the girl who had known me before I knew myself. I married her and built a life with her. I walked across stages, first as a high school graduate, then again as a college graduate. Each step forward felt like a step away from the past, a deliberate refusal to let history repeat itself.

I have had multiple careers, not because I was lost, but because I've searched for the right place to plant my roots. I trusted God to guide me, to show me where I needed to be. And He has.

We are able to afford a decent home; not just four walls and a roof, but a place of safety, of comfort. A place our son will never have to be ashamed of. A place where laughter fills the rooms instead of silence thick with unspoken pain.

I am the father I never had. I am the husband I always wished my mother had. I understand the weight of love, the responsibility it carries, and I do not take it lightly.

I am still far from perfect and fall short of God's glory daily.

I made it out.

Brother five had a different kind of struggle.

By the time he came along, our grandparents had softened. The years had worn them down, reshaped them. Where once there was strictness, there was leniency. Where once there was discipline, there was indulgence.

They thought they were being kinder. They thought they were doing better. But in their efforts to be gentle, they left him unprepared for the world outside our home.

He was never allowed to struggle. Never given the chance to fail and figure out how to rise again. If there was an obstacle, someone moved it for him. If there was a challenge, someone solved it before he even had to try.

He was handicapped, but not in the way Brother three was. His wounds weren't visible. His scars weren't physical. But they were there, just as deep, just as lasting.

Because when life finally demanded that he stand on his own, he had never learned how.

For years, he lived within the limits that others set for him, dependent on a disability check that barely covered more than survival. The world told him he couldn't, so he believed it. The system made it easy to settle, so he did.

But there was always something in him that wanted more.

He graduated high school when some thought he wouldn't. He was daring enough to try college, even when doubt whispered that he wasn't built for it. He has always cared deeply, loved fiercely, and wanted success just as much as the rest of us. The only difference was, he didn't know how to fight for it.

And for a long time, he didn't.

Then something shifted.

Maybe it was time. Maybe it was maturity. Maybe it was watching the rest of us stumble forward, seeing that there was a way out after all. Whatever it was, it lit something in him that hadn't been there before.

He reached out. He tried again.

And now, as I write this, he has recently gotten his driver's license. He has his own apartment at twenty-seven. He is watching me closely—not with envy, but with intent. He is studying my steps, taking notes, and trying to understand what it takes to break free.

I am so proud of him.

He is trying to get out.

Brother six feels abandoned. And the truth is, he probably is.

I was the one who raised him when no one else would. The one who made sure he ate, who sat with him through homework, who shielded him from the worst of what life threw our way. I stood in the gap because I had to. Because someone had to.

But in my desperation to escape, to carve out a life beyond the walls that had confined me for so long, I left him behind.

I didn't mean to. I didn't want to. But that doesn't change the fact that I did.

Now, there is a rift between us that I don't know how to close. It cuts deep, deeper than words can fix. Sometimes, I wonder if I will ever be able to reach him again and if he will ever stop seeing my success as proof of his own isolation.

But I pray.

I pray that one day when he looks toward me and Brother five, he won't see abandonment. He will see hope.

I pray that something will stir in him. He too will take that next step, get his license, find a job, and discover training or schooling that sparks something in him. I pray he will believe, even for a moment, that his future doesn't have to be a reflection of his past.

I pray he gets out.

I still remember the exact moment I held my first real paycheck in my hands. I was seventeen, standing in the break room of the small store where I had been working, my fingers gripping the thin slip of paper like it was a golden ticket. Up until that point, I had only done odd jobs, mowing lawns for neighbors, hauling furniture for a few extra bucks, whatever small gigs I could get. Those jobs never paid much, and even when they did, I never saw the full amount. My uncle, who had helped me find the work, always took a cut, saying it was to cover gas money or whatever expense had come up that week. I didn't complain. That was just the way things were. But this? This paycheck was mine. All mine.

For the first time in my life, I felt a sense of financial independence, however small it might have been. It wasn't just about the money. It was about what it represented. Proof that I had worked for something and earned it. A small step toward standing on my own two feet. I held onto that feeling for as long as I could, savoring it, imagining all the ways my life could change now that I had an income of my own.

But it didn't take long before my brothers noticed.

One of them was twenty-three at the time. He had been struggling to keep a steady job, always bouncing from one thing to the next, never quite settling. When he found out I had gotten paid, he came to me, a casual grin on his face, and asked if I could spot him some money for tobacco. Just a little, he said. Just this once.

I was seventeen, barely scraping by, still figuring out how to manage my own expenses. And yet, here he was, looking to me for help. I remember staring at him, feeling a strange mix of emotions, surprise, frustration, and maybe even a little resentment. But most of all, I felt something new settle over me, something heavy and unshakable.

That was the moment I first felt the weight of the coat of many colors on my shoulders.

It wasn't about the money. It was about what it meant. About the way my family, my own older brother, had started looking at me differently. I wasn't just the younger brother anymore. I was someone they could lean on. Someone who, despite barely getting started in life, was already expected to carry a weight I hadn't asked for.

And from that moment on, I knew this was just the beginning.

It was at that moment that I began to see the similarities between myself and Joseph from the Bible. From the outside, it may have seemed like I had been handed favor, like I had been chosen for something greater while the rest of my family was left behind. Maybe to them, it looked effortless, as if doors simply opened for me while they remained locked for everyone else. But that wasn't the truth.

The truth was that I had worked for everything.

Nothing had ever come easy. I refused to let my circumstances dictate my future. Even when I was kicked out at seventeen, even when I had nowhere to go and spent time homeless, I still got up every morning, went to school, and refused to let my grades slip. I knew that if I let myself fall, no one was going to catch me. I had to be the one to keep pushing forward, to find a way through the struggle, even when it felt like I was doing it alone.

Of course, that never made sense to them.

To them, I wasn't struggling. I was just different. And in their eyes, different was the same as being favored. They didn't see the nights I spent wondering how I would make it to the next day, the exhaustion of carrying responsibilities I hadn't asked for. They didn't see the choices I made, the sacrifices, the discipline it took to keep going. All they saw was the outcome. And to them, that was enough to believe I had been given something they hadn't.

But I knew the truth. Favor had nothing to do with it. It was never about luck or being chosen. It was about the fight, the perseverance, and the refusal to let my story be written by anything other than my own determination.

Why not just give up?

That thought has crossed my mind more times than I can count. There were nights when I lay awake, exhausted down to my bones, wondering if it was even worth it. It would have been easier to stop pushing, to stop fighting for something different, to just accept the life I was born into. Easier to give in, to let myself believe that this was all there was, and all there would ever be.

But at the end of the day, we all choose our hard.

It's hard to wake up at 5:30 AM every morning, drag yourself out of bed when every muscle in your body screams for more sleep, and force yourself to go to the gym. But it's also hard to be severely overweight, struggling to make it up a flight of stairs, battling knee pain and back pain with every step. It's hard to be disciplined with your money, to say no to things you want so you can save and invest in your future. But it's also hard to be broke, constantly stressed about bills, and stuck in a cycle where there never seems to be enough.

Both paths are difficult. The difference is in which struggle you choose to live with.

My brothers chose their hard, just like I did. But the difference was that mine led to a future they couldn't yet see. While they saw obstacles as reasons to stop, I saw them as the price of admission for something better. They thought I was lucky. They thought I had been given something they hadn't. But the truth was, I was just willing to endure a different kind of pain—the pain of growth, of sacrifice, of walking a road that didn't promise immediate rewards.

And that's the thing about choosing your hard. One of them keeps you stuck. The other moves you forward.

To them, my choices were strange. They couldn't understand why I was so determined to go to school every day, why I refused to let my grades slip, why I distanced myself from the things that held them back. From their perspective, it looked like I had been handed some special favor, like I was wrapped in a coat of many colors that set me apart. But what they didn't realize was that I was simply making different choices—ones that wouldn't pay off until years down the road.

I have always seen those choices as a glimmer of hope in a dark cave. With every difficult decision I made as a teenager, I took another step forward, moving closer and closer to breaking through the darkness. I knew that if I just kept going, if I stayed the course, I could live a life entirely different from anything my family had ever known.

Reader, be sure to help me educate the younger folks on this concept called *delayed gratification*. It means making small sacrifices now that will add up to bigger rewards in the future. It's the difference between spending every dollar you earn or saving a little bit each month so you can buy something meaningful later. It's choosing to study when your friends are out partying because you know the grades you earn now will open doors in the future. It's saying no to temporary pleasure in exchange for long-term success.

Against their better judgment, my siblings eventually had to acknowledge what they had known all along. I was cut from a different cloth.

I may have been born into the same family, but one day, I would create my own. And it would look nothing like the one I came from.

For years, they teased me for the very things that set me apart. They mocked the way I spoke, always telling me I was trying too hard to sound proper. They called me out for acting differently, for refusing to participate in the same destructive cycles they clung to. But now, those same choices they once ridiculed had started to make sense to them.

Sometimes, it's almost funny to hear them speak so highly of me when I'm around, only to hear later about the things they say behind my back.

Reader, I tell you this to warn you. If you haven't witnessed this up close yet, you probably will.

People don't always understand when someone chooses to take a different path, to go against the grain they were raised in. They will be laughed at. They will be questioned. And when they finally start to succeed, they may be resented for it.

I encourage you to be so focused, so driven, and so passionate about your mission that you don't let these bumps in the road derail the youth you are called to serve. I encourage you to help that young person push against the grain. I encourage you to admire the people who seem a little strange, the ones who don't fit in. Those are often the people who change the world.

I encourage you to wear your own coat of many colors.

And if you've already found yours, maybe it's time to help someone else find theirs.

Escaping at a Cost

I went from having a relationship with poverty to being married to the idea of escaping it. And the worst part? I can't even apologize for it.

For years, I didn't just live in poverty—I made a home in it. I sat with it, let it shape the way I thought, let it whisper to me that this was all I would ever know. I wallowed in it, convinced that struggling was just part of my identity, something I had to accept rather than something I could fight against. It weighed me down, kept me stuck, and made me feel like no matter how hard I tried, I would always end up right back where I started.

But the moment I finally escaped, something in me snapped. I made a silent vow to myself, one that felt less like a promise and more like a survival instinct. I would never go back. No matter what.

That kind of mindset comes with a cost.

And I don't know if it's a price I will ever be able to pay fully.

Maybe it's because of how I grew up, but I never formed deep emotional ties. That may sound strange, but let me explain.

When you spend years in survival mode, constantly calculating how to make it through the next day, relationships become secondary. There's no room for vulnerability when you're focused on making sure you have a place to sleep or food to eat. Attachment feels like a luxury, something other people can afford but you can't.

So I built walls. I kept my distance. I learned how to be self-sufficient, and how to rely on no one but myself. And now, even though I'm no longer struggling the way I once was, I find myself wondering if I've paid too high a price for my escape.

Because while I may have freed myself from poverty, I sometimes wonder if I also locked myself into something else.

I was abandoned at an early age. Left to figure out life on my own long before I should have had to. And with that kind of beginning comes baggage, the kind of weight that sits on your shoulders no matter how far you try to run from it. It lingers in the way you think, in the way you move through life, in the decisions you make before you even realize why you're making them.

In my house, every conversation revolved around money. Or more specifically, the lack of it.

There was never enough. Not for the bills. Not for groceries. Not for the little things that other kids took for granted, like school trips or birthday presents. My grandfather never tried to hide his fears about making it from one month to the next. I saw the worry on his face, etched into the lines on his forehead, sitting heavy in his tired eyes. I heard it in his voice every time he checked the mail, hoping there wasn't another overdue notice inside.

When growing up in a house where money is a constant source of stress, you don't have to be told you're a burden. You feel it. You carry it. It probably didn't help that we were often reminded of the financial burden we kids placed on the family structure. To this day, I still find it humorous that each of us placed a financial burden, but we also helped pay the bills with the checks mamaw received for being our guardian. Our grandfather was always weighing if we were more of a credit or debit, and we were well reminded of it.

I decided early on that I would never let my future family feel that way.

I wanted to thrive. Not because I craved luxury or status, not because I wanted to flaunt success or prove anything to anyone, but because I never wanted my children to hear the kind of conversations I did. I never wanted them to lie awake at night, listening through thin walls, wondering if they were the reason there wasn't enough money that month.

So I ran.

I distanced myself. I worked. I fought for something better. I refused to look back.

And in doing so, I left casualties behind.

Maybe it was selfish. Maybe it was survival. Maybe it was both. When spending your whole life trying to escape something, you don't stop to think about what or who might be left behind in the process.

My baby brother relied on me for years. I was the one who made sure he had food when there wasn't much to go around. I was the one who helped him with his homework, who shielded him from the weight of the world as much as I could. He looked up to me in ways I didn't fully understand back then. Maybe you're in a similar situation. Maybe there's someone in your life who depends on you the way he did me. Someone who sees you as their anchor, their safe place, their proof that something better exists.

But when you're drowning, it's hard to be someone else's lifeline.

I was so consumed with getting out that I convinced myself I had to leave everyone behind. I told myself that if I wanted a real shot at something better, I couldn't afford to stay. And maybe I was right. It's a whole lot easier to climb out of a pit when you're not trying to carry others on your back. It's a whole lot easier to run when you're not dragging someone alongside you.

But even after I left, even after I carved a new path for myself, he was still there. He was still the little boy I had practically raised before I left at seventeen. And no matter how far I ran, I couldn't forget that.

So, after I graduated from college a semester early, I came back.

I didn't just want to help him. I needed to help him. He was only twelve years old, still just a kid, and I knew that if I didn't step in, the cycle would continue. I had seen it happen too many times. I had lived it. And I wasn't about to let it happen to him.

I thought that maybe, just maybe, I could guide him toward something better. I thought that maybe I could be the person I needed when I was his age.

But I was too late.

Every step I took to help him escape poverty was met with resistance. It didn't matter how much I wanted it for him. He was just a kid, a sponge soaking up everything in his environment. The life I wanted to pull him out of was the only one he had ever known. The instability, the struggle, the way money always ran out before the month did—it was normal to him. It was home.

I begged him to stay with me at the house I was renting. I wanted to give him structure, stability, and a glimpse of something different. I thought if he could just experience a life where he didn't have to worry about the things we worried about growing up, maybe he would start to want it for himself. Maybe he would believe it was possible.

But structure wasn't something he had ever been given. Growing up without it, the idea of it can feel more like a cage than a lifeline.

So he fought against it.

He pushed back at every turn, resisting everything I tried to offer him. No matter how much I explained, no matter how much I tried to show him another way, I couldn't break through. I wanted so badly for my brother to see what I saw. To understand that there was a different way to live. But I was just one voice against an entire reality that told him otherwise.

The real problem was that I was fighting a battle I had no real support in. My grandparents never stepped in to help reinforce what I was trying to do. And looking back, I don't know why I expected them to. They had already raised seven of their own children. Then they raised me and my five brothers. And even now, years later, my Mamaw is raising three of her great-grandchildren.

They were simply tired.

Tired in a way that went beyond just needing rest. Tired in a way that made them resigned to the cycle, accepting of it, maybe even numb to it. I think part of them had stopped believing in escape a long time ago. And if you don't believe in something, how can one possibly teach it to someone else?

Tired of parenting. Tired of struggling. Tired of fighting a battle they had long since accepted they would never win.

Why would any twelve or thirteen-year-old choose structure and discipline over complete freedom? Why would he pick curfews, responsibilities, and rules when he could stay up all night, sleep all day, and do whatever he wanted without consequence? He wouldn't. And he didn't.

I don't hold it against my grandparents.

They never found their own way out of poverty, so how could they have led someone else? They did what they could with what they had. But I couldn't keep trying to save someone who didn't want to be saved.

After years of trying and failing miserably, I finally made the hardest decision I had ever made.

I let go.

I told myself that if my brother ever wanted help, he would have to come to me and ask for it. I could no longer carry the weight of trying to pull someone out of poverty when they weren't willing to take the first step themselves.

I had to protect my own future.

And more than that, I had to protect my marriage.

My wife, my best friend, had not signed up to raise a twelve-year-old straight out of college. She had married me, not the responsibility I refused to put down. And as much as I hated to admit it, constantly worrying about my brother was starting to take a toll on us.

Was it tough for him? Absolutely. Was it unfair? Without question. But poverty does not care.

You can fight it. You can hate it. You can pray and cry yourself to sleep at night. But no matter how much it's wished away, you still carry it with you.

And my brother, now a high school graduate, still carries it with him.

He doesn't know what to do with his future, and instead of doing *something*, he is doing *nothing*. Every time I try to reach out, every time I offer to mentor him or help him figure out his next steps, I am met with resistance. The resentment runs too deep.

I clawed my way out, and he still hasn't forgiven me for it.

I can't fully explain why people who are raised in the same environment- facing the same struggles, turn out so differently. There is no perfect formula, no single moment that determines the outcome.

The only explanation I can offer is that when I had nothing and no one else, I ran toward my Heavenly Father and everything He had to offer me. I crashed hard.

And thankfully, I crashed straight into the arms of a loving Father.

I didn't just stumble into faith. I ran toward it, desperate for something bigger than myself, something more than the life I had known. And when I did, I found that my Heavenly Father had been waiting for me all along, arms open, ready to pull me out of the pit I had been living in. He offered me grace, direction, and the opportunities I had once believed were out of reach.

Some, like my siblings, run in the opposite direction.

Just as I spent years clawing my way out of shame and self-pity, some run just as fast and just as hard into despair.

The truth is, there are a lot of *double failures* in this world. Let me explain.

There are people who fail to meet the expectations of the world around them. And in some cases, that can actually be a good thing. Most people don't get up at 5:00 a.m. to go to the gym. Most people don't track their meals or push themselves beyond what is comfortable. The ones who do are often the ones who rise above.

But what happens when someone fails to meet society's expectations and also their own?

Maybe you thought you would be further along by now. Maybe you always assumed you would graduate college, find success, and build a life that looked nothing like the one you came from. But here you are, working a job you never planned on, stuck in a cycle you never imagined for yourself.

You become a double failure in your own eyes and in the eyes of the world.

And once that doubt creeps in, once that weight settles on your shoulders, it's easy to sink into self-pity. It's easy to let yourself believe that this is all there is. That you are a victim of your circumstances and there is no way out.

But I'm here to tell you, there is.

I want to end this chapter with a reminder: it is okay to mourn who you used to be. Growth often requires sacrifice, and sometimes, that sacrifice is the version of yourself that once felt familiar and comfortable. It is okay to acknowledge that the person you were had to fade away for you to step into the person you were meant to become.

Transformation is not just about change; it is about surrender. It is about letting go of the old patterns, old mindsets, and old versions of yourself that no longer align with the future you are building. It can be painful. It can feel like loss. Because, in many ways, it is. The old you is gone. Your desires have shifted, your priorities have changed, and the path you once thought you would follow may no longer exist.

Not everyone will understand this transformation. Some people will try to hold on to the version of you that made sense to them. Some will resist your growth because it challenges their own comfort. And that is okay. You are not meant to stay the same just to make others comfortable.

Because the ones who embrace transformation fully and unapologetically are the ones who shape the world. They are the ones who step into their purpose with courage. They are the ones who inspire change, break cycles and redefine what is possible. And if that means letting go of who you once were, then so be it. The future is waiting.

Genesis 37:23 (KJV) "And it came to pass, when Joseph was come unto his brethren, that they stript Joseph out of his coat, his coat of many colours that was on him."

PART TWO

MOVING TOWARD
A SOLUTION

Chapter 7:

TYPES OF POVERTY

I fully understand that not everyone is born into poverty like I was, and for that, I'm grateful. No child should have to start life at a disadvantage, struggling for things others take for granted. But when you really think about it, isn't it sad that we feel the need to celebrate something that should be the norm? A child being born into a stable home with a loving mother and father, a roof over their heads, and parents who can afford to meet their needs shouldn't be seen as a luxury or an exception. And yet, in today's world, that has become the dream. Stability, security, and opportunity are not given; they are privileges.

But poverty isn't just about money. It's easy to think of it as simply the absence of financial resources, and while that's certainly a major factor, I want to challenge that narrow view. Poverty wears many faces, and it exists in places we might not expect.

I was introduced to this idea by a few churches and one of my mentors. They taught me that financial poverty, the one we most commonly recognize, might not even be the most damaging. There are other forms of poverty that can rob people of fulfillment, direction, and even their very sense of self.

In this chapter, I want to explore these different types of poverty. While this book primarily focuses on financial struggle, it would be a disservice to ignore the others. Spiritual poverty, purpose poverty, and stewardship poverty can be just as debilitating, if not more so, than financial lack.

Let's dive into what these mean and how they impact people in ways that money alone cannot fix.

Spiritual Poverty

Someone like my son, born into an upper-middle-class family with access to everything he needs, could still be suffering from poverty. That may sound contradictory, but poverty is not always financial.

There are people who seem to have it all—money, success, and stability—yet they cry themselves to sleep at night. They feel lost, heartbroken, and burdened by addictions. Their suffering isn't visible in their bank accounts, but it runs deep in their souls. This is spiritual poverty.

The reality is that even the people closest to us will eventually fail us. No matter how much they love us, they are human, and humans are imperfect. But there is one person who will never fail you. He promises that He will never leave you, that you are not forgotten, and that you are not forsaken.

Earlier in this book, I touched on the topic of religion. Religion has become a politically correct blanket that people wrap themselves in, something they identify with rather than something they live by. But I want to take a different path, a narrower road. The cure for spiritual poverty is not found in religion; it is found in a relationship with Jesus Christ.

The Bible tells us in Romans that no one is perfect except God and His Son and that all have fallen short of His glory. It also speaks of a sin debt that must be paid, one so great that no amount of money could ever cover it. That is a concept many fail to grasp before it is too late. There is only one way for this debt to be paid, and that is through Jesus.

But what does that really mean? It means surrendering your life to Him. It means choosing to follow Him, even though you will still make mistakes and fall short. It means being unashamed to call yourself a child of God and recognize that, through Jesus, you are an heir to something greater than anything this world can offer.

The Bible tells the story of a rich man in the book of Luke who failed to understand this. He had everything the world could give him, but he lacked the one thing that truly mattered. I pray that you do not make the same mistake.

Purpose Poverty

Maybe you weren't born into financial poverty. Maybe you have accepted Jesus as your Savior and found freedom from spiritual poverty. But what about purpose? Have you ever considered that poverty can also exist in the form of an unfulfilled life?

God has a purpose for you. He designed you with intention, created you for a reason, and placed you in this world with a role to play. But not everyone finds that purpose, and many live their lives never walking in it.

Both financial and spiritual poverty can make it difficult to pursue your God-given purpose. When someone is financially struggling, survival becomes the priority. Their thoughts are consumed with making ends meet, putting food on the table, and keeping a roof over their head. It is hard to focus on anything beyond the weight of daily survival.

Spiritual poverty creates a different kind of struggle. Trying to serve God's purpose for your life without a relationship with Him is like hiking an unfamiliar trail with countless forks in the road and no map to guide you. You may stumble onto the right path by chance, but you won't move efficiently, and your impact will be limited.

Purpose poverty leaves people wandering, searching for meaning in places that will never truly satisfy them. Wealth and success cannot fill that void. Even good intentions and hard work are not enough without the guidance of the One who created you. True fulfillment comes when you align your life with God's plan and step boldly into the purpose He has set before you.

Stewardship Poverty

We are entrusted with many things in this world, and among them, time is perhaps one of the greatest gifts God has given us. In Genesis, God set the ultimate example by creating the universe and then choosing to rest on the Sabbath. We are called to do the same.

It's interesting to observe how people who have risen from poverty manage their time. They've escaped the monotony of endless minimum-wage jobs and the constant chase for overtime, which is commendable. But are they making the best use of the extra time afforded to them by upward mobility? Are they spending this time with their families, engaging in activities that promote their well-being, such as exercise?

I challenge you to reflect on this, dear reader. Are you glorifying God in how you use your time? Are you being a good steward? Would you say you are rich in your stewardship, having been faithful over the little things that, over time, add up to be significant?

This is a type of poverty I must continually guard against. It's easy to become consumed with the fear of losing the position you've gained, especially for those who have escaped financial poverty. However, it should be more concerning to lose quality time with the family you've been blessed with, such as your spouse and children. I've found that many middle-class high performers who have escaped poverty face this challenge regularly. If this resonates with you or someone you know, I encourage you to remember what truly matters in this world.

God has given us simple commandments: love yourself, love your neighbor, and He has a purpose waiting for you. My purpose is to help older adolescents escape their family's cycle of poverty by loving them, treating them with dignity, and sharing my story of how, with God's help, I made it out. Find a purpose in life that brings you joy.

Consider a husband and wife married for sixty years; when the wife passes away, the husband often follows not long after. This phenomenon, known as the "widowhood effect," indicates that in the first six months after losing a spouse, widows and widowers are at a 41% increased risk of mortality[7]. Purpose gives us life and makes life worth living.

Years ago, Daisha and I started the "Little" scholarship in our hometown of Inez. As I tell the high school scholarship recipients each year, I encourage you to find your purpose, make a difference, and give back.

2 Corinthians 8:9 (KJV) "For ye know the grace of our Lord Jesus Christ, that, though he was rich, yet for your sakes he became poor, that ye through his poverty might be rich."

Chapter 8:

MOVING FROM A SURVIVALIST MINDSET

W e were nearly taken away from our mother due to a lack of food. Like newborn children, all we knew was food, milk, and love … we craved it. Our whole world revolved around it. Hunger consumed us, shaping our thoughts, our actions, and even our relationships. We were nearly trapped in that state forever. But more than food, we craved love and affection, something we often had to go without.

Psychologist Abraham Maslow referred to this as the foundation of the Hierarchy of Needs, a theory that explains human motivation and development. At the very base of this pyramid are physiological needs; food, water, warmth, and rest, without which a person cannot focus on anything else.[8] I came dangerously close to never developing past this level. Had my life continued in this state, my mind would have remained fixated solely on survival, incapable of reaching for anything greater. When all you can think about is where your next meal is coming from, there is little room to dream, to plan, or to grow.

I remember vividly how desperate we were. When a cake of cornbread hit the table, my brothers and I would claw and scratch and fight … anything to secure our share. It was the same with soup beans, spaghetti, or store-bought pizza. It was every man for himself. The idea of sharing, of being considerate, or of showing compassion was out of the question. We were survivalists.

Many members of my family still are.

I am incredibly grateful that I made it out. That I broke free from this elementary level of thinking, this primal need-driven existence. But it wasn't easy.

When your mind is consumed with meeting basic needs, there is little room for anything else. You cannot think about others, you cannot dream about the future, and you certainly cannot love the way Jesus did.

Survival mode keeps you trapped in a cycle where every decision is reactive rather than intentional.

This mindset can manifest in daily routines, too. The small, seemingly insignificant decisions we make each day—what to wear, where to place our keys, what to eat—can drain our mental energy. If we don't structure our lives efficiently, we end up spending valuable time and focus on trivial matters. The key to breaking free from a survivalist mindset is to create systems that free up mental space for higher-level thinking.

For example, it is best to plan your next day the night before. Lay out your clothes before bed so you don't waste time deciding in the morning. Keep your shoes and keys in the same place every day so you don't have to search for them. Even eating the same meals or following a structured routine can help reduce unnecessary decision-making.

When you move from a survivalist mindset to a productive, creative thought process, you unlock a greater potential. By automating the little things in life, you create space for bigger, more meaningful decisions. And in doing so, you shift from simply surviving to truly living.

Now, what does it actually look like when you have "made it?" I'd like to warn you because I truly believe that many of you readers will reach this potential, or you may help someone else reach it if you are a teacher, coach, mentor, parent, or a loved one investing in another. I encourage you to warn the person that you are investing so heavily in.

You see, one day, they may move from a survivalist mindset to potentially having everything they ever wanted. They no longer struggle for their next meal. They now have the mental capacity for growth. But I can honestly say there comes a shock.

Let me first say I'm not preaching a prosperity gospel here. They will still struggle. I am referring to simply having the basic needs of an individual or a family met. That person will finally get to a point where they can just breathe and have room for the growth that we have been referring to. So, I encourage you to help them fill that space with healthy things.

The natural tendency will be to fill it with fear. You see, there's a fear that comes with escaping poverty. You end up getting everything that you dreamt of—everything that everyone else had in their basic lives—

so you are filled with fear and panic about how to move from a survival mindset to a prosperous one. There is a phase two, if you will, to escaping poverty. It is keeping someone from crashing their lives. Similar to addiction, really, one needs to learn time management. They need to learn biblical teachings of how to manage wealth and how to move from one mindset to another. Encourage them to love people as Christ did.

Jesus tells the parable of the Good Samaritan in Luke chapter 10. A Jewish man was traveling from Jerusalem to Jericho when he was attacked by robbers, stripped of his clothes, beaten, and left for dead. A priest passed by and ignored him. A Levite also passed by and did nothing. But then a Samaritan, someone from a group despised by the Jews, stopped to help.

Not only did the Samaritan tend to the man's wounds with oil and wine, but he also placed him on his own donkey, took him to an inn, and cared for him. The next day, he gave the innkeeper money and promised to cover any additional costs to ensure the man's full recovery.

This is the essence of going the extra mile. The Samaritan didn't just provide momentary aid—he followed through, ensuring the man was truly restored.

In the same way, when helping someone transition from poverty, we shouldn't just assist them in the moment. We must also walk with them through the next stage, ensuring they don't fall back down. It's not enough to provide temporary relief; we must invest in their long-term success.

Warning Against a "Me" Mentality

When someone has spent years fixated on their own survival, it is no surprise that they struggle to think about anyone else. When you are constantly in fight or flight mode, your world shrinks. Your focus narrows to one thing, getting through the day, the week, the month.

Have you ever met someone who cannot stop talking about themselves? Someone who fills every conversation with I and me statements? Maybe they crave attention. Maybe they take credit for work they barely contributed to. Maybe, no matter what the situation is, they always manage to paint themselves as the victim.

This is someone suffering from a me mentality.

And here is the hard truth. This mindset does not just hurt them. It pushes people away. It drains relationships. It limits opportunities.

We all have moments of self-focus, but if you want to grow, if you want to build real connections and create something meaningful, you have to shift your mindset. You have to recognize that the world does not revolve around you.

Do not be the person who makes everything about themselves. Be the person who listens, who contributes, who lifts others up instead of just looking out for their own survival. Because the truth is, no one truly thrives alone.

People with a me mentality will crush progress before it even has a chance to grow. They are so hyper fixated on themselves that collaboration becomes impossible. No one wants to work with them. No one even wants to be around them for long.

Can you tell I have met a few of these people? I am sure you have too.

But here is the thing. We cannot entirely hold it against them. They just never moved up Maslow's hierarchy of needs[9]. They are stuck at the base level, worrying about self rather than having the center approach of loving others and considering their needs.

They are trapped in survival mode, focused on securing their own needs first, making sure they are okay before they ever consider anyone else. And for some, that is as far as they ever get.

They never shift to a mindset of growth, of connection, of building something greater than themselves. They never reach the point where they can love others fully or genuinely consider the needs of those around them.

But we are not meant to stay stuck at the bottom. We are meant to move beyond survival, to step into a life that is not just about self-preservation but about purpose, about giving, about lifting others up. That is where true fulfillment is found.

I encourage you to embrace a "we" mindset because that is where true transformation happens. When we shift our focus from "me" to "we," we create space for growth, collaboration, and revelation. The world does not change because of one person working alone. It changes when people come together, lifting one another up, sharing wisdom, and supporting a greater purpose.

Even Jesus, who carried the full power of God within him, never made it about himself. He did not seek personal recognition or claim credit for his miracles. Instead, he always pointed to the Father, showing us the power of humility and unity. If the Son of God himself embodied a "we" mentality, how much more should we strive to do the same?

When you adopt this mindset, you will notice something remarkable. People will be drawn to you because they will see someone who values teamwork, who listens, who shares, and who uplifts others. Relationships will deepen, and doors you never expected to open will begin to unlock.

On the other hand, a "me" mindset, the belief that success is a solo journey, often leads to the opposite of what you hope for. It creates isolation rather than connection. It builds walls instead of bridges. It leaves you stranded on an island of lost opportunities, wondering why things are not working out as you planned.

But the good news is that you always have the choice to shift your perspective. You can start today by looking beyond yourself, inviting others in, and choosing to see success as something best achieved together. When you do, you will find that the most meaningful victories are the ones shared.

One of the greatest gifts you can give yourself is the ability to choose. Options create freedom, and freedom allows you to build the life you were meant to live. Poverty was so painful because it left me feeling trapped, backed into a corner with no clear way out. I grew up in an environment where relying on the government was the norm and where dreams of education and financial independence felt distant, almost impossible. There was no roadmap, no guidance, just survival.

What changed my life was expanding my options. Strengthening my faith, developing an entrepreneurial mindset, pursuing education, and seeking out mentors gave me opportunities I never thought I would have. With each step forward, my world grew bigger. I started to see beyond the limitations I had been taught to accept.

I am not naïve enough to believe that change happens overnight. Breaking free from a poverty mindset is not a quick fix. It takes time, sometimes years, to undo the habits, fears, and beliefs that keep people stuck. I know because it took me well into my twenties to truly break free. It was not just one thing that helped me escape. It was all of it combined—a strong support system, faith, education, a willingness to take risks and be vulnerable, and the wisdom of mentors who had already walked the path ahead of me.

Poverty does not just affect finances. It affects the way you see yourself and the world around you. It teaches you to think in terms of scarcity instead of abundance. It makes you focus only on survival, leaving little room for generosity, growth, or long-term vision. But when you start expanding your options, you begin to shift from a mindset of lack to a mindset of possibility.

My prayer for you is that you find your way out of any limiting beliefs that keep you stuck. I pray that you experience the kind of freedom that allows you to love others fully, just as Christ did and still does. You were not meant to live in survival mode. You were meant to thrive, to grow, and to give the same gift to others. Keep pushing forward, keep expanding your options, and trust that God has more in store for you than you can even imagine.

Ephesians 2:10 (KJV) "For we are his workmanship, created in Christ Jesus unto good works, which God hath before ordained that we should walk in them."

Chapter 9:

GOD'S GRACE

There was so much to unpack about my relationship with my grandfather. It is a collection of raw, torn emotions that still haunt me today. For years, I harbored a deep resentment toward him. I hated him fiercely because our interactions were defined by conflict. We constantly bumped heads, and he could never understand why I refused to settle for the life I was born into. His words and actions stunted my growth, hindered my ability to build meaningful connections, and crushed my creativity and confidence. He would belittle me for wanting to dress well or simply for caring about my appearance. In many ways, I felt as though he had stolen my childhood.

He imposed strict limitations on our lives. Not only was I not allowed to spend time with friends or local entrepreneurs—people who might have broadened my horizons—he even forbade me from playing sports. In his mind, our world was meant solely for survival: shelter and food were enough. Imagine living in a household with six children where sports, play, or any kind of creative freedom was off the table. That was the norm for us.

His treatment extended into every aspect of our daily lives. He laughed at my struggles with depression, dismissing them with the cold logic that he had faced far worse in his life and that I should simply "suck it up." My compassion, which I considered a strength, was mocked by him. He often labeled me a sissy and a cry baby, and his communication was dominated by yelling. If he wasn't shouting, he was speaking in harsh tones that left no room for understanding or comfort.

One of the most ironic memories is that he sang in church throughout my entire life. Despite his many flaws, he managed to belt out a tune with a force that could command a room. It is a reminder that even the most conflicted individuals can possess a spark of beauty amid their struggles.

His habits defined the environment of our home. He smoked heavily, chewed tobacco, and drank coffee with an almost religious devotion. In our house, these three became a sort of unholy trinity. Every week, he and mamaw would each go through roughly a carton of cigarettes. I can't help but think about the money spent on tobacco and coffee, money that might have been used for something beneficial, like buying basketball shoes for us. And then there was the issue of our water. The quality in Martin County was notoriously below average, and he refused to use tap water for making coffee. Yet, we were all forced to drink that water daily, a constant reminder of where the rest of the family stood in priorities.

He was constantly stressed over finances, an obsession that permeated every aspect of our household. His anger and yelling were frequently tied to the struggle to make ends meet. He never offered us a word of encouragement or a pat on the back for even the smallest success. For him, success meant paying the monthly electric bill and avoiding high-interest loans from local loan sharks, a harsh reality for someone poor and from Appalachia, where such traps were all too common. Academic achievements were never celebrated, a neglect that may have contributed to my two oldest brothers never graduating.

Yet, despite all the negativity and limitations he imposed, my grandfather also saved us. As mentioned in a previous chapter, there was a time when Child Protective Services were about to take us away. It was only a matter of time before the system intervened. I will always be grateful for his role in keeping us together and ensuring our survival despite the many hardships.

I can't help but wonder what life would have been like if he hadn't been there. Perhaps we would have been split up, and I might have found myself with a family that nurtured upward mobility from the start. Or maybe things would have ended much worse. Both possibilities seem possible, and the uncertainty only adds to the complexity of my feelings about him.

He introduced us to Jesus Christ. For that, I am most grateful. I wouldn't say I was happy about being forced to go to church, but I can't deny that it exposed me to the Word of God early and often in life. Without my relationship with God and His Son, Jesus, who knows where I would have ended up? Maybe I would have followed through on the dark thoughts of harming myself at a young age. But God's love and affection saved me. Changed me. Kept me.

We laughed occasionally. He wasn't always a monster. He was human, imperfect, just like the rest of us. There were moments, scattered and rare when we shared something good. He had Jesus in him; I believe that. He just battled a lot of demons, demons from his past, from his choices, and from the overwhelming burden of raising us all. He wasn't without his softer moments. He let us ride in his lap and pretend to drive as kids, gave us the occasional chance to play pool as we got older, and even allowed us to join him in watching wrestling if we kept quiet.

Despite never having received an apology or any of the calls "just to check in" or congratulations that I referred to earlier in chapter five, God gave me peace about my relationship with my grandparents, specifically my grandfather. I've often heard that, "Time heals all wounds." I can honestly say it took far more than time for me to be able to forgive my grandfather. It took the power of God and the reminder of what his son Jesus went through for us, even after how we treated him, for me to offer him the grace he did not deserve. Being a few years removed from his presence also helped, I'm sure. So, I decided to start calling and visiting them. Probably not as much as I should have, but just because God allowed me to forgive didn't mean that I had forgotten all the pain.

Later in life, when he received his cancer diagnosis and after we had reconciled, I took him to a live WWE event and shared a meal of Mexican food with him. There aren't many things that us folks in eastern Kentucky prioritize over these two. In all seriousness, that day marked the first time we spent quality time together, just the two of us, a significant step up from the county fair wrestling events he was used to attending. The beauty of adulthood has led me to stop waiting for others to create the relationships I want and to take ownership within myself and make those happen. Remember, I always wanted to have a healthy father-son relationship with him. Despite these moments of connection, his focus remained largely on survival. Toward the end of his life, I had learned to love him exactly how he was, even with his faults, and tried to see him how God does.

He did his best with us, I think. He struggled with poverty in every way imaginable, financially, emotionally, and spiritually. His past was marked by drugs, alcohol, theft, and even time in jail. As a young man, he got caught up in the world of car thievery in inner Chicago. But somewhere along the way, he turned his life over to Jesus Christ. That decision led him to Pike County, Kentucky, where, at the age of forty-five, he met my mamaw and began the second chapter of his life.

For a time, he and the family thought he had won his war against cancer. Turns out, he had only won a minor battle. The disease came back with a vengeance, and in 2023, it took him. He fought hard, spending months in and out of the hospital. But as the cancer spread, his organs began shutting down. When the family called to say he was in bad shape and that I should come to see him before it was too late, I didn't hesitate. After all, we had already reconciled, and I had come to love him, even if it was from a distance.

That night, I rushed to the hospital to find a frail shadow of the man I had despised for most of my life. It was clear he didn't have much time left. Bedfast, barely able to whisper one-word answers, refusing to eat or drink, he was slipping away. And for the first time in my life, I wasn't angry at him. Not even the tiny bit that my flesh kept hidden away. The love of Christ had traveled to my innermost being and ripped it away. I just saw a man at the end of his road, worn down by life, yet still clinging to the faith that had saved his soul all those years ago.

After I walked into the room, he sat up straight. His eyes widened, and he instinctively fixed his shirt, almost as if he wanted to present himself properly. Then, in a voice stronger than it had been in days, he spoke:

"Joebear, my boy."

Joebear. The name my family had always called me.

That was the only time I heard him call me his boy, and now, just days before the end of his life, those words carried a weight I never expected. At that moment, something shifted. For the first time in a long time, he looked at me not with criticism or disappointment, but with warmth. And as if my presence had given him a second wind, he did something he hadn't done in days, he ate. A full plate of food.

For the next few hours, he answered my yes-or-no questions, mostly about wrestling, his favorite escape. He seemed energized, as if just seeing me had breathed life back into him. I could tell he was surprised that I had come, that I had CHOSEN to be there. But isn't that what grace, mercy, and forgiveness are all about? Freely offered to those who, by human standards, might not deserve it. I was no better than him. Again, pointing you back to the cross of Jesus, we all fall short of his glory.

I encourage you to do the same. Freely offer love and forgiveness not just for others, but also for yourself. You might just be surprised by the peace you encounter. Something only God can do.

A few days later, I was preparing to leave for a three-day work event when my brother sent a message. Gramps had taken a turn for the worse and was back in the hospital. The doctors told us to call the whole family in. I rushed to his bedside, but this time, he wasn't sitting up, he wasn't eating, and he wasn't speaking. His eyes were closed, his breathing shallow, the ventilator doing the work his body could no longer manage. A few hours later, he was gone.

Although we weren't related by blood, he was the only grandfather I had ever known. I never met my father's parents, and mamaw's first husband had passed before I was old enough to know him.

Reader, sometimes, the people in our lives who don't seem to understand may simply not know any better. We are all shaped by the world we grew up in—for better or worse. Our grandfather often spoke of the hardships he had faced as a child. He was abused. He was socialized into a harsh reality, one that left scars he carried his entire life.

He never allowed oats in the house. The smell alone enraged him. As a child, he had been forced to eat them, but not before someone had urinated in them. He and his twin sister had been made to endure that cruelty. He didn't talk specifics about his past often, but when he did, it was clear: he had not been merely whipped for misbehavior. He had been beaten. Fiercely.

I don't share this to excuse him, but to understand him. To see the full picture.

Sometimes, distance is necessary. Sometimes, reconciliation can only come after time apart—years, even. But if there's one thing I've learned, it's that people can change, even if only in their final days. The man who had once been so hardened, so closed off, softened before the end. And now, no matter what came before, I will always remember the way he looked at me in those last days and called me - *"My boy."*

Romans 3:23 (KJV) "For all have sinned, and come short of the glory of God."

Chapter 10:

PROGRESS OVER PERFECTION

E scaping poverty is about so much more than a silver bullet solution. There is no single moment of breakthrough, no magic wand that transforms life overnight. If that were the case, solving poverty would be as simple as handing someone suffering from financial hardship a lump sum of money. But in most cases, that money would be gone in no time, and they would find themselves right back where they started or, in some cases, even worse off.

That is because money alone does not fix poverty. It does not undo the deeply ingrained habits, thought patterns, and generational cycles that keep people trapped. Poverty is not just a lack of resources. It is a mindset, a way of thinking and living that shapes the choices people make. Simply injecting money into the situation without addressing the underlying issues will only provide temporary relief, not lasting change.

A real escape from poverty requires something much deeper. It takes a complete shift in thinking, a willingness to change behavior, and a relentless commitment to progress, even in the face of setbacks. It means learning financial discipline, developing skills, seeking education, and surrounding yourself with people who challenge you to grow. It requires breaking free from the scarcity mindset that keeps people living day to day without a plan for the future.

This process is not easy, and it does not happen overnight. It takes time to unlearn old habits and replace them with new ones. It takes effort to develop the discipline to manage money wisely, make strategic decisions, and build something that lasts. But those who commit to the process, who push through the challenges, and who refuse to settle for where they started will see change happen over time. While the road may be difficult, the good news is that change is possible for anyone willing to put in the work. Step by step, choice by choice, progress will come. It tests your resolve in ways you never expected, pushing you to your limits and often making you question whether breaking free is even possible.

For many families, poverty is not just a temporary struggle. It is a generational cycle that has persisted for decades, sometimes centuries. It is passed down like an unwanted inheritance, an heirloom that no one asks for, but few manage to escape. It is woven into the fabric of daily life, influencing decisions, opportunities, and even the way people see themselves and their potential. When poverty has been in a family for that long, it does not simply disappear with a single job offer or one smart financial decision. The roots run deep, tangled in mindset, habits, and circumstances that make escaping it incredibly difficult.

It is also important to understand that even after you have fought your way out of poverty, you will not suddenly transform into a flawless, idealized version of yourself. Life does not work that way. Growth is not a straight line, and the past does not simply vanish once you reach a certain level of stability.

Old habits do not disappear overnight. They linger in the background, waiting for moments of weakness to resurface. I am more than a decade removed from my own struggles, yet I still catch myself slipping into patterns that once held me back. I still find myself settling for the bare minimum when I should be pushing for more. I still wrestle with self-doubt, questioning my potential even when I have proven myself time and time again. There are days when discouragement creeps in, whispering that I am not capable enough, not worthy enough, not strong enough.

There are moments when the weight of responsibility feels overwhelming, and I wonder if it would be easier just to stop trying. To stop pushing so hard. To let go of the expectations and simply exist without constantly striving for something better. But then I remind myself of the truth. I am not chasing perfection. I am chasing progress.

Escaping poverty is not just about changing your financial situation. It is about changing the way you see yourself. It is about breaking not just external barriers but also the internal ones that have kept you thinking small for so long. It is about learning to silence the voice that tells you to settle, to stop, to give up.

Progress is not about never falling. It is about getting back up every single time.

One book that has profoundly shaped my perspective is *Atomic Habits* by James Clear. One of the core ideas he explores is that *best is the enemy of good*[8]. It is a concept that has stayed with me because it speaks to a deep truth about human behavior. We often become so obsessed with achieving perfection that we end up doing nothing at all. We set impossible expectations for ourselves, and when we inevitably fall short, we retreat. We procrastinate. We make excuses. Instead of focusing on small, consistent improvements, we become trapped in a cycle of overthinking and inaction.

I like to take Clear's idea a step further by highlighting the difference between being in motion and taking action. It is easy to mistake one for the other. Being in motion feels productive. You are planning, researching, organizing, and preparing. It gives the illusion of progress. But none of that actually moves you forward until you take real action.

James Clear explains that we often choose motion because it is safe. It allows us to feel like we are working toward something without exposing ourselves to failure. But the hard truth is that motion without action is just another form of procrastination. No amount of preparation will replace the moment you decide to act. Progress does not come from endlessly planning. It comes from making a decision and following through.

This mindset shift has been a game-changer for me. It has made me more conscious of the moments when I am simply staying busy rather than actually moving forward. Now, whenever I feel stuck, I ask myself a simple question: Am I taking action, or am I just in motion? The answer is often the difference between staying where I am and making real progress.

I encourage you and the people you have the privilege to influence, to become people of action, not just people in motion. Take the first step, even when you don't feel completely ready. Move forward, even when you know mistakes are inevitable. Growth does not come from waiting for the perfect moment. It comes from doing, learning, and adjusting along the way.

And most importantly, embrace the truth that there is always room for improvement. No matter how far you've come, no matter how much you have accomplished, there is always another level of growth waiting for you. There is always more to learn, more to refine, and more to build.

Progress is not about getting everything right the first time. It is about moving forward consistently and intentionally. It is about choosing growth over comfort, persistence over hesitation, and action over endless preparation.

Progress over perfection. That is the key to lasting change.

"Pull Yourself Up by Your Bootstraps"

It is a common phrase, right? One that gets repeated whenever the topic of poverty comes up, as if it holds the ultimate solution. But let's pause for a moment and really think about what it means.

What exactly are bootstraps? Where are they? How does someone physically pull themselves up by something attached to their own boots? And perhaps the most pressing question is, what if someone does not have boots to begin with?

This phrase assumes that everyone starts from the same place, with the same resources, opportunities, and support systems. But the reality is far more complicated. Some people are born into families that can offer stability, guidance, and financial security. Others start with nothing. No safety net, no access to quality education, and no connections that could open doors. For them, the idea of simply pulling themselves up is not just unrealistic, but it dismisses the real struggles they face.

Escaping poverty is not just about effort. It is about opportunity. It is about access. It is about breaking cycles that have existed for generations. Telling someone to pull themselves up by their bootstraps without considering whether they even have boots in the first place ignores the depth of what it truly takes to change one's circumstances.

Hard work matters. Determination matters. But so do systems that create opportunities and communities that offer support. Instead of repeating phrases that oversimplify struggle, maybe the better question is, how do we make sure that everyone has the boots they need to take that first step forward?

The idea that anyone can succeed simply by working hard and staying determined is a comforting one. It suggests that success is within reach for anyone willing to put in the effort. But in places like Appalachia, where poverty has been deeply rooted for generations, the truth is far more complex. Hard work is essential, but it is not always enough.

For many living in these communities, the barriers to success are not just personal but systemic. Jobs that offer a livable wage are scarce. Education opportunities are limited. Access to healthcare is often unreliable. Public transportation is nearly nonexistent in rural areas, making it difficult for people to reach better-paying jobs even if they are willing to travel. Generational poverty does not just mean a lack of money. It means a lack of connections, mentorship, and sometimes even basic necessities.

Some might hear the phrase "pull yourself up by your bootstraps" and scoff, not because they have a lack of desire to improve their lives, but because they are starting with so little. How do you pull yourself up when the boots were never there to begin with? What happens when you are stuck in a cycle where your parents struggled, their parents struggled, and no matter how hard you work, it feels like the deck is stacked against you?

That is not to say that people do not try. Many work themselves to the bone just to survive. They take on multiple jobs, stretch every dollar, and do everything in their power to provide for their families. But without access to education, affordable housing, healthcare, or a support system, breaking free from poverty is not just difficult. It can feel impossible.

The problem is not a lack of ambition or effort. It is a lack of resources. A child growing up in a well-funded school with teachers who encourage them to dream big will have a vastly different path than a child in an underfunded district and an underfed belly. A person born into a family with financial stability has the freedom to take risks, pursue passions, fail, and try again. Someone who grows up in survival mode does not have that privilege. When every dollar matters, when missing a shift could mean missing a rent payment, there is little room for trial and error.

The idea of self-reliance is admirable, but it should not be used to dismiss the very real obstacles that keep people trapped in poverty. Success is not just about pulling harder on the bootstraps. It is about making sure that everyone, no matter where they start, at least has a pair of boots.

Poverty is not just about lacking money. It is about the weight of uncertainty, the exhaustion of never knowing if tomorrow will be any better than today. It is easy to say, work hard, and you will make it. But what happens when someone works hard every single day and still cannot afford the basics? What happens when they cannot even think about buying a sturdy pair of boots because rent, food, and survival come first? This is where the real conversation about poverty begins.

There is no magic formula for escaping poverty. The stories of sudden success, of people pulling themselves up by sheer willpower, often leave out the parts that matter most. The opportunities, the support systems, the lucky breaks. Hard work matters, but so does access. So does consistency. So does the ability to keep showing up, even when it feels like nothing is changing.

That does not mean personal responsibility is irrelevant. It just means the conversation needs to shift. Instead of telling people to pull themselves up by their bootstraps, maybe we should be saying, wear whatever you have and keep being a person of action. If you do not have boots yet, use what you do have. If you do not have a job, keep showing up at the places where opportunities exist. If you do not have a home, keep showing up at school, at the library, or at the places that can help you build something, no matter how small.

I know this because I lived it. I know what it is like to walk into school after not having a roof over your head all night until God finally opens a door a few hours before the first bell rings, to show up to class pretending everything is fine when the weight of survival sits heavy on your shoulders. But I also know the power of consistency. Even when it felt like nothing was improving, every single step forward mattered. Every class I attended, every assignment I turned in, every connection I made. It all added up in ways I could not see at the time.

Poverty does not disappear overnight. But progress happens in the small, steady choices. It happens in the moments when you decide to keep going, even when the odds are stacked against you. Sometimes, it starts not with a pair of boots, but with the determination to walk forward regardless.

I remember one of my professors during my first year of college saying something that stuck with me. He stood at the front of the lecture hall, looked around at all of us, and said, "Guys, passing this course really is not that difficult. Seventy percent of it is just about showing up." At the time, it sounded almost too simple, but the more I thought about it, the more I realized how true it was.

Earning a degree or certification is not just about intelligence. It is not just about your background or even financial stability. It is about proving that you have the discipline to keep going. It is about pushing through exhaustion, frustration, and setbacks. It is about being present and accountable, even on the days when you do not feel like it, even when you are not sure if it will make a difference.

That lesson goes far beyond college. Success in almost anything is rarely about giant leaps. It is not usually about one life-changing opportunity or some big breakthrough moment. It is about the small, consistent steps that add up over time. It is about the effort that no one sees, the work that does not feel rewarding in the moment, and the times when you keep going even when progress feels slow.

It is not about pulling yourself up by some imaginary bootstraps. It is about waking up every day, putting on whatever shoes you do have, and taking another step forward, even when it is hard. Even when it feels like nothing is changing. Because, in the end, the people who make it are not always the smartest or the most privileged. More often than not, they are the ones who simply refuse to stop being a person of action.

Be the Someone

Too often, we sit back and wait, assuming that someone else will step in. We tell ourselves that there are people out there who are more qualified, more experienced, or simply better suited to handle the situation. We convince ourselves that it is not our place to interfere, that it is not our responsibility to carry. And while we hesitate, while we stand on the sidelines, there are people, especially young people, struggling right in front of us. Some of them are searching for guidance. Some just need support. Others may simply be hoping for a kind word to remind them that they are seen.

Maybe you are a teacher who has been in the system for years. You have watched student after student slip through the cracks, and over time, you have grown numb to it. You are underpaid, overworked, and tired of feeling like your efforts do not make a difference. You tell yourself that no matter how much you care, the system is too broken to fix. You stop fighting because it is easier that way. But then there is that one student, or maybe a few, who reminds you why you started in the first place. They have potential. They have a spark. But life keeps throwing obstacles in their way. You see it, clear as day, yet they cannot see it for themselves. They just need someone to invest in them. Someone to take them under their wing. Someone to believe in them before they even believe in themselves.

I know this because that was me. And not just once. Not just with one mentor or one person who decided to step in. I needed that support again and again. I needed people who refused to stand back and watch me struggle alone. I needed people who saw something in me when I could not see it myself.

The truth is, we all have the power to be that person for someone else. To step in instead of stepping back. To remind someone that they matter, that they are not invisible, and that their future is not set in stone. Because sometimes, all it takes is one person who cares enough to show up.

This chapter is for teachers, coaches, pastors, public figures, entrepreneurs, and anyone who has made it out, but may have forgotten what it was like to struggle. If you have reached a place of stability, take a moment to remember that your journey was not a solo effort. Somewhere along the way, someone extended a hand to you. Maybe it was a teacher who saw past your rough edges and pushed you to keep going. Maybe it was a coach who refused to let you quit, no matter how frustrated you felt. Maybe it was a pastor who took the time to listen when no one else did. Maybe it was a mentor who recognized something in you that you could not yet see in yourself.

It is easy to move forward in life and forget what it felt like to be on the other side. The struggle, the uncertainty, the feeling of wondering if you would ever make it. But now that you are here, now that you have overcome, you have a responsibility to reach back. You have a responsibility to challenge the low ceiling that society has placed on the people within your circle of influence. Do not just accept it. Challenge it. Break it. Refuse to let it define what is possible for those who are still fighting to find their way.

Every single day presents an opportunity to make an impact. It does not have to be a grand gesture. A single conversation can plant a seed of confidence. A moment of encouragement can shift the way someone sees their future. There are children, teenagers, and young adults all over the world who are thirsting for an opportunity. Give them a drink. They are searching for someone who will believe in them, believe in them. Someone who will tell them that they are capable, tell them. Someone who will remind them that their circumstances do not have to define them, be the reminder.

You have access to a fountain. You just need to be willing to offer a cup because many kids cannot yet reach the water.

I know this to be true because I was one of those children. I had intelligence, I made decent grades, I had charisma, and I was respectful. But I lacked. I lacked guidance, direction, and the steady hand of someone who could help shape my future. I was like a diamond in the rough, buried beneath the weight of circumstances I did not create. I needed someone willing to see past the surface and take the time to polish what was already there.

Potential is often like a well of oil hidden deep beneath the ground, waiting to be discovered. It does not reveal itself easily. It takes effort to dig. It takes patience to extract. But the reward of finding and refining it is immeasurable.

The best coaches do not just see talent; they nurture it, refine it, and challenge it to grow. Great teachers do not just present information; they inspire curiosity and resilience. Pastors, when led by the love of Christ, do not just preach; they shepherd, they invest, they uplift. True mentors do not focus on imperfections; they focus on possibility. They see what can be, even when the person in front of them cannot.

The world does not need more people who sit on the sidelines, waiting for greatness to reveal itself. It needs more people who are willing to dig, willing to invest, and willing to believe in those who are still struggling to believe in themselves.

I encourage you to invest. Invest in the life of a young person who may never be able to pay you back. Invest in the quiet kid sitting in the back of the classroom who is afraid to raise their hand. Invest in the teenager who always seems on the verge of giving up but secretly hopes someone will notice. Invest in the young adult who has the drive but lacks the direction.

Be the *someone* they need. Because sometimes, all it takes is one person to change the course of a life forever.

I am reminded of the story of how David became king in the Bible. When God sent Samuel to anoint the next king of Israel, he was told to go to Jesse and choose one of his sons. From a human perspective, the choice seemed obvious. Jesse had strong, impressive sons, the kind of men people expected to lead. But God did not choose the biggest or the most powerful. He chose the last son, the one no one had even thought to bring forward. David was out in the fields, tending sheep, unnoticed and overlooked. Even his own father did not consider him a likely candidate for greatness.

Yet God saw something in David that no one else did. He saw a shepherd who would one day lead a nation. He saw beyond what was visible and recognized the potential hidden beneath the surface.

That is what it means to invest in someone. It is about looking past what is immediately obvious and seeing what could be. It is about recognizing the greatness in someone long before they can see it in themselves. It is about stepping into the role of a guide, a mentor, a supporter, and helping them move toward the future they were meant to have.

David was not perfect. His life was filled with mistakes and missteps, but God still used him in a mighty way. That makes me wonder how many kings and queens are lying dormant among our youth, just waiting for someone to see them. How many are waiting for someone to acknowledge their worth, their potential, and their capacity to lead and create change?

Be the *someone* who sees.

I am grateful for the people who invested in me. This goes beyond mentorship, though mentorship is important. What I am talking about is deeper than guidance or advice. It is about your mindset, your perspective, your heart. It is about choosing to live a life that matters, one that seeks to uplift others and make a difference in ways that may seem small at first but leave a lasting impact.

I think back to a moment that changed me forever. I was a young teenager, just beginning to take my relationship with Jesus seriously. I wanted to seek Him more, to worship Him in spirit and in truth. One night, I attended a church service with a family member. I sat in the middle of the church, quietly singing along with the hymns when an elderly woman turned to me.

You have just the best voice, she said warmly. Then, she asked me to go to the front of the church and sing a song.

I was shy. I was not used to standing out, so I politely declined. But instead of simply nodding and turning away, she looked me in the eye and spoke words that have stayed with me ever since.

"God has great plans for you, young man", she said. "I do not know exactly what, but you were made for great things."

That was it. A brief conversation with a stranger, a few simple words, but they planted a seed in me. She had no idea who I was, and I never even got her name, but what she said gave me something I had not fully had before, an expectation to live up to. A belief that I was meant for more. As I reflect on those words now, I realize they planted a truth that would carry me through so much of my journey. For many years, I thought I was supposed to build something better for myself, to strive for success and fulfillment. But the elderly lady's words, "God has a plan for your life," were a reminder that this pursuit wasn't just about what I could achieve on my own. They pointed me toward the bigger picture—that the success I sought was meant to align with God's purpose for me. What she spoke to me was not just an encouragement to strive for greatness but a reminder that greatness, in all its forms, was part of a divine plan that was already unfolding. That realization has always stayed with me, guiding me toward a future I could never have imagined on my own.

She was the *someone* for me.

She didn't have to say what she did. She didn't have to take the time to encourage me. But she chose to, and that choice made an impact that has shaped my life ever since.

Reader, be bold. Be intentional. Be the someone.

Delayed Gratification

Delayed gratification is the ability to resist an immediate reward in favor of a greater reward in the future. It sounds simple in theory, but in reality, it is one of the hardest skills to master, especially for those who have grown up in financial hardship.

When money is scarce, survival takes precedence over everything else. The idea of waiting for something better later feels like a luxury when the present is uncertain. There is no room to think about long-term gains when the immediate concern is putting food on the table, keeping the lights on, or making sure rent is paid. In these situations, the future feels distant and unpredictable, while the needs of the present are urgent and unavoidable.

For many, financial struggles shape their mindset from an early age. When you grow up watching your parents stretch every penny and make tough choices between essentials or go without, you internalize the idea that money should be used as soon as it comes. Saving for later doesn't always feel like an option because "later" has never felt guaranteed. This is why people who have experienced financial instability often struggle with the concept of delayed gratification. It's not because they lack discipline or don't understand the benefits—it's because their experiences have taught them that waiting isn't always a safe bet.

When every paycheck feels like a lifeline, it's difficult to think about investments, savings, or opportunities that take time to mature. The urgency of the present outweighs the potential of the future. Even when financial stability improves, the habit of prioritizing immediate needs over long-term goals can linger. Learning to delay gratification requires not just financial security but also a shift in mindset—one that allows a person to trust that the future will be stable enough to wait for.

It takes time, patience, and sometimes unlearning survival-based habits to embrace delayed gratification. But when done intentionally, it can lead to greater financial freedom, opportunities, and a sense of control over one's future.

This mindset is completely understandable, especially for those who have lived through financial hardship. When someone has spent years struggling to make ends meet, the idea of waiting for a greater reward later can feel impractical or even impossible. However, this way of thinking often creates a cycle of poor financial and life decisions that can be difficult to break.

Payday loan companies and high-interest lenders take advantage of this struggle. They market themselves as a quick fix, offering immediate cash that feels like a lifeline in a moment of need. The relief is instant, but it comes at a cost. Steep interest rates, hidden fees, and repayment terms often keep borrowers trapped in a cycle of debt. What starts as a solution quickly becomes another problem, making it even harder to break free from financial instability.

Beyond finances, the inability to delay gratification affects many areas of life. It can lead to impulsive decisions that provide short-term satisfaction but long-term regret. In education, it might mean skipping opportunities to learn or develop skills because they do not offer immediate rewards. In health, it can result in choosing comfort over consistency, such as opting for fast food instead of cooking, skipping workouts, or avoiding necessary medical checkups. In relationships, it might mean prioritizing instant validation over the effort required to build meaningful, lasting connections.

Delayed gratification is difficult, but it is often the key to long-term success. It requires trust in the future and the discipline to make sacrifices today for something better tomorrow. Learning to apply this concept across different areas of life, whether in financial planning, career growth, personal development, or well-being, can make all the difference. It is not about denying yourself happiness in the present but about making choices that lead to greater stability, fulfillment, and freedom in the long run.

Education. Many people choose quick money over further education because the long-term rewards feel too distant. Growing up, I saw this firsthand. After high school, many of my classmates skipped college or trade school to take high-paying jobs in the coal mines. At 18, earning $60,000 to $100,000 a year seemed like the best option.

But short-term gain doesn't always mean long-term security. The coal industry declined, and many of those who had chosen immediate income over further education found themselves unemployed with no backup plan. They had no degrees, no trade skills, and no easy way to transition into other fields.

Education requires sacrifice. It means putting in years of effort before seeing the reward. But those who invest in learning—whether through college, apprenticeships, or technical training—often gain more stability in the long run. While it may seem like delaying success, it is actually building a stronger foundation for the future.

Sex. Society often encourages instant gratification when it comes to sex. The focus is on pleasure in the moment, without always considering the long-term consequences. But sex comes with responsibilities—emotional, physical, and even financial.

Many relationships fail because they are built on attraction rather than true connection. Some people rush into commitments or move in together too soon, hoping that immediate closeness will create lasting security. But when the foundation is weak, relationships often crumble.

Delaying gratification in this area means being intentional—choosing partners wisely, building emotional connections before physical ones, and making decisions based on long-term goals rather than immediate desires.

Food/ Exercise. Health is another area where delayed gratification plays a huge role. Eating unhealthy foods provides instant pleasure, but the long-term consequences—weight gain, poor health, and low energy—are often ignored until they become serious.

One unhealthy meal doesn't make a person overweight, just like one workout doesn't make someone fit. But over time, repeated choices add up. Fast food, sugary snacks, and processed meals may be convenient and satisfying at the moment, but they often lead to long-term health issues.

Making better food choices requires patience. It means prioritizing nutrition over cravings, choosing home-cooked meals over fast food, and sticking to healthy habits even when the results aren't immediate.

Money. Financial stability is one of the biggest areas where delayed gratification matters. Many people struggle with money not because they don't earn enough, but because they prioritize immediate spending over long-term savings.

Payday loans, credit cards, and pawnshops thrive on this mindset. People borrow money to cover short-term wants, not realizing how much more they will owe in the long run. A $500 loan can quickly turn into a $1,000 repayment because of interest and fees.

The same applies to impulse spending. Buying the latest phone, designer clothes, or a new car may feel good at the moment, but if it means living paycheck to paycheck, the long-term consequences can be severe.

Financial success often comes down to discipline—saving instead of spending, investing instead of wasting, and choosing long-term security over short-term pleasure.

Work. Many people chase the highest-paying job immediately rather than thinking about long-term career growth. This often leads to job-hopping, lack of skill development, and an unstable financial future.

A minimum-wage job might not seem appealing, but sometimes, it's a stepping stone to something greater. People who commit to learning, improving, and growing within a company often rise through the ranks, while those who chase quick cash often find themselves stuck in the same cycle years later.

Building a career takes time. It requires patience, consistency, and, sometimes, starting from the bottom. But those who think ahead and put in the effort often find more stability and success in the long run.

Substance Abuse. Drug addiction is one of the most destructive examples of instant gratification. The high is immediate, but the long-term consequences are devastating. People turn to substances for quick relief from stress, anxiety, or emotional pain, not realizing that each time they do, they are deepening their dependency.

Addiction is a cycle that can feel impossible to escape. It often starts innocently—just a drink here, a pill there, or maybe something to help ease the stress of the day. What begins as occasional use slowly turns into a habit, and before you know it, it becomes something you rely on just to get through the day. At first, it feels like a quick fix, a way to numb the pain or forget the struggles. But over time, your body and mind start craving the substance, not because you want it, but because you need it just to function.

What many don't realize is that addiction doesn't solve anything. It doesn't make your problems go away. In fact, it only delays facing them, and the longer it continues, the worse those problems become. The momentary relief it offers quickly fades, leaving behind more confusion, more hurt, and more pressure than before. You start losing sight of who you were, and the substance becomes the only thing that feels like it's holding you together.

Addiction traps you. It locks you in a vicious cycle where every high is followed by a low, and every escape leads you back into a deeper hole. The more you try to numb the pain, the bigger the problems grow, and eventually, it feels like you're fighting an endless battle. It's not just about the substance; it's about the emptiness and fear that you're trying to fill, and it takes a lot more than willpower to break free. But it's possible, and sometimes the first step is realizing that you deserve more than just surviving. You deserve to live fully, to face your challenges head-on, and to break free from the cycle that holds you captive.

Recovery, on the other hand, is the ultimate form of delayed gratification. It requires patience, self-control, and endurance. The process is slow and often painful, but in the end, it leads to true freedom.

Philippians 3:12-14 (KJV) 12 Not as though I had already attained, either were already perfect: but I follow after, if that I may apprehend that for which also I am apprehended of Christ Jesus. 13 Brethren, I count not myself to have apprehended: but this one thing I do, forgetting those things which are behind, and reaching forth unto those things which are before,

14 I press toward the mark for the prize of the high calling of God in Christ Jesus.

Chapter 11:

MENTORSHIP

I lacked it my whole life. It was like wandering through a vast desert, desperate for a drop of water. I craved it. I needed it. And then, one day, I found it.

For the longest time, my survival strategy was simple. I just did the opposite of what everyone around me was doing. I saw the cycle of bad decisions, the way people seemed trapped in the same patterns, and I wanted no part of it. I knew God had more for me. But the hardest lesson I learned was that He never just made everything better in an instant. This life is not a sprint. It is a marathon. A long, grueling journey where progress comes in small, stubborn steps. Along the way, I picked up bits and pieces from different people, fragments of wisdom, moments of clarity, and slowly, I started putting them together.

Where I grew up, we didn't get out of the holler much. Our world was small. I never met many professionals or saw what success looked like up close. Occasionally, I would cross paths with wealthy folks, but they were usually elderly and had inherited their fortune. I never got the chance to see how someone actually became successful. What did it mean to be a professional? How did they get there? These questions haunted me throughout my childhood. I simply couldn't picture that kind of life.

We were too busy figuring out where our next meal was coming from to think about career paths. But I longed for guidance. I wished, with everything in me, that someone would take me under their wing. Just one person was willing to give me an example to follow. Someone who would look past the holes in my clothes, past the last name that carried no weight, past the family that seemed to set a low ceiling over my life automatically. I just wanted to be seen. Not for where I came from, not for what I lacked, but for my potential. I didn't beg for money. I begged for an opportunity. I begged for mentorship.

I have spent my entire life being a sponge, soaking up everything around me. When I was younger, I had no father to teach me how to regulate my emotions. No mentor to show me the ropes of life. No one ever pulled me aside to tell me what was socially acceptable or how to carry myself in certain spaces. I had to learn through trial and error, sometimes painful, always embarrassing.

I will never forget the moments that shaped me. The first time I showed up to a dinner in basketball shorts and a muscle shirt, completely unaware of how out of place I looked. The way people stared. The way I wanted to disappear. I didn't know. I had never been taught. I had to figure out on my own that athletic socks don't go with dress shoes, that ordering food at a sit-down restaurant isn't as simple as pointing at a menu, that a drive-thru isn't just about grabbing food. It is about knowing what you want before you reach the speaker so you don't hold up the line.

Drafting a professional email. Tying a tie. Knowing which fork to use at a formal dinner. These were things other kids learned from their parents, their mentors, and their environment. I learned them the hard way, piece by piece, mistake by mistake.

And yet, despite it all, I kept going. I kept absorbing. I kept learning. Because deep down, I knew that mentorship, even if I had to find it in bits and pieces, would be the key to breaking the cycle.

I am deeply grateful for my time at a small private Christian college tucked away in the rolling hills of Appalachia. It was more than just a school. It was a place that stretched me, shaped me, and opened my eyes to a world I had never truly seen before. It was here that I first began to understand what it meant to carry myself as a professional.

I remember the feeling of stepping into my first etiquette class completely out of my element. I had never thought about how to confidently enter a room or the small but significant details that set professionals apart. I wasn't just being taught how to dress the part—I was being required to live it. At least one day a week, I had to show up in professional attire. That meant no worn-out jeans, no sneakers, no hoodies. It was intimidating at first, stepping into dress shoes that felt unnatural and stiff, or buttoning up a collared shirt that felt foreign on my skin. But with time, I adjusted. I started to see that these small changes weren't just about appearance. They were about discipline. They were about stepping into a version of myself I had never met before.

At that college, there was a phrase I heard often: "The leaders are here." At first, it sounded like just another slogan, something the administration said to inspire students. But over time, I began to believe it. The structure of that place gave me something I had never really had before—boundaries, expectations, and a belief that I had something to offer. Coming from a place where life was unpredictable, where the future felt more like a question mark than a destination, that structure was vital. It gave me direction. It gave me confidence. And most importantly, it gave me my first real glimpse of mentorship.

I won't lie; there were moments when I nearly walked away. The pressure to conform to this new world, the overwhelming sense of being out of place, it almost broke me. My first semester was the hardest. I thought about quitting more times than I could count. But then something changed. The president and vice president of the college took an interest in me. They weren't just distant authority figures. They were from the same world I had come from, raised in Martin County, Kentucky, just like me. They knew what it meant to grow up in a place where opportunity felt scarce. And yet, they had made it. They had climbed the ladder. They had pushed past the same obstacles I faced and had come out on the other side.

Their belief in me made all the difference. Sometimes, they would ask me to stop by their office, and those small conversations became moments of guidance. Other times, they would invite me to speak at college events, pushing me into spaces where I never thought I belonged. Slowly, I started to believe that maybe I did belong. Maybe I was capable of more than I had ever imagined. Just before graduation, I was awarded their family scholarship—a moment that hit me with more weight than I expected. It wasn't just about the money. It was about what it represented. These two men had seen me. They had recognized something in me that, for most of my life, I had struggled to see in myself.

They had come from the same struggles I had. They had faced the same doubts. And yet, they had built something for themselves. Maybe just maybe, I could too.

Years later, I would return to higher education, not as a student, but as an administrator. I started as the Financial Aid Director, stepping into a role I never imagined I would hold. Not long after, I replaced my supervisor and took on even more responsibility, overseeing both Financial Aid and Admissions. I still struggle to wrap my mind around it sometimes. The kid who once doubted whether he'd even make it through college was now running two major departments within one.

Of course, it wasn't without challenges. I made mistakes along the way. I was young and still finding my way professionally. Thankfully, I had built strong relationships with my mentors, and their guidance had opened doors for me. But I also knew that I had worked for it. I had pushed myself further than I ever thought possible. And yet, I wanted more.

I remember sitting down with my two mentors, the men who had once helped me find my footing, and asking them a simple but important question: How can I progress? Their answer was direct. If I wanted to be taken seriously by my peers, if I wanted to continue moving forward, then I needed to further my education.

So I did. I enrolled in a Master's program, determined to prove that I belonged. I poured everything I had into it, pushing myself harder than ever before. Eleven months later, I completed a program that was supposed to last two years.

Looking back, I see how mentorship shaped my journey. I see how the right people, at the right moments, changed the course of my life. And I see how, without them, I might have walked away from it all.

Professional Mentorship

We are all sponges. My journey, just like yours and the youth you serve, is an ongoing process of soaking in knowledge, absorbing experiences, and continuously striving toward becoming a true professional. The pursuit of professionalism, I've learned, isn't just about mastering a skill or reaching a title. It's about growth, resilience, impact, and the ability to adapt when life throws unexpected opportunities your way.

One such opportunity came when I was thrust into the fire of professional development, an experience that left me not burned, but refined. When I left the college to join a new organization, I initially found myself in a role assisting with sales and marketing. It didn't take long for me to realize that this wasn't my calling. However, I understood that even in the wrong place, there were valuable lessons to be learned. I held onto the belief that God had called me to this organization for a reason, and I remained open to discovering what that purpose truly was. Similar to the concept of being on the right bus but wrong seat found in Jim Collins' book *Good to Great*[10].

Interestingly, the company also had an education division, which immediately seemed like a better fit for my background in higher education. It felt like a natural transition, and I anticipated that in time, I would find my way there. Just when I was closing in on an opportunity to make that shift, something unexpected happened, something that could only be described as divine intervention.

At a large company event, I was busy helping with recruitment efforts when a chance encounter changed the course of my career. As I was refilling candy bowls, one of those seemingly mundane tasks that professionals often overlook, but can put you in the right place at the right time. Aaron Burr, from the musical Hamilton, would say I was in the room where it happens. I noticed the Founder and CEO of the organization. He was engaged in conversation with the individual I had hoped would become my new supervisor, someone with whom I had previously had brief discussions about possibly joining the college division. However, in the weeks leading up to the event, those conversations had gone quiet.

I was beginning to feel frustrated, uncertain if my aspirations were being considered or if I had misinterpreted my path altogether. Then, as I passed by again, the CEO stopped me and asked if I had a minute to talk. How could I say no?

He led me to a quiet spot in the arena, away from the bustling crowd of thousands. As we sat overlooking the event, he asked me a series of questions: How long had I been with the company? Did I enjoy my role? And then, he addressed the elephant in the room—would I be interested in joining the college division if the opportunity presented itself?

Without hesitation, I answered honestly. "Yes, I feel that may be where God is leading me."

I braced myself for his reaction, worried he might see this as a betrayal. After all, I had been hired for a specific job, and here I was, only a few months in, expressing interest in an entirely different path. Instead, his response took me completely by surprise.

He nodded thoughtfully and said, "Okay, you could potentially do that one day, if the timing works out and all. Or you could come to work directly with me in my office."

I tried to play it cool, but internally, I knew my eyes had widened, and my excitement was barely contained.

The CEO went on to explain that the role didn't come with a formal title or a set list of responsibilities, but one aspect stood out: mentorship. He spoke about the importance of having someone he could trust to oversee projects across all divisions, including education, as the company grew. Someone who could also help drive him to events so he could focus more on the mission side of the business. But more than that, he emphasized that this role would equip me with tools and relationships that would be valuable no matter where my career took me.

I was stunned. Here was someone who had already achieved a significant level of professional success, yet he was genuinely invested in my future. He wasn't just offering me a job. He was offering me growth, mentorship, and an opportunity to build something meaningful.

I took a couple of weeks to think and pray about the offer. It wasn't a decision to make lightly. Looking back now, I can confidently say that it was one of the best decisions I've ever made. God was faithful through it all, guiding my steps even when I wasn't entirely sure where they would lead.

And along the way, I picked up more than just career insights. I even learned that when attending a professional dinner, cutting my entire steak at once is not the best etiquette. Growth comes in all forms.

There are hidden rules to professional classes. Bridges Out of Poverty discusses how when moving up to a new class, it is beneficial to have a relationship with someone already in that class because they understand these unspoken rules[11]. Hidden rules are typically kept secret, allowing members of higher-level classes to identify outsiders.

For example, if you walk into a football game only knowing basketball rules, you won't last long. The same applies in the professional world—if you have a weak handshake, avoid eye contact, dress poorly, or display unfamiliarity with professional etiquette, you immediately stand out as an outsider. These signals act as red flags to upper-class professionals.

We all need mentors. If you see someone struggling to navigate these spaces, consider stepping up to guide them. This is where building social capital becomes crucial, allowing individuals to seize opportunities that would otherwise remain out of reach.

Spiritual Mentorship

The Bible gives clear instructions on certain responsibilities, one of which is to care for widows and orphans. I understood the orphan side of this well, having almost been one myself. But widows? That was something I had to learn about.

I found guidance from an elder deacon at Inez Freewill Baptist Church. The church's name is significant because I discovered this wisdom in Appalachia, a region often overlooked when it comes to structured mentorship and upward mobility.

He taught me that caring for widows wasn't just about offering condolences or checking in once in a while. It was about truly being there, stepping into the quiet spaces of their lives where loneliness had settled in. He took me along when he visited the sick and elderly in our church and community. Some of them were in hospitals, some in nursing homes, and others in houses that had long since stopped feeling like homes.

There were the shut-ins, the ones who couldn't leave their homes anymore. I learned how something as simple as reading them a church bulletin or praying with them could remind them they were still a part of the congregation. I watched as my mentor greeted them not with pity but with warmth, as if they had just stepped into the church sanctuary themselves. He made sure they knew they were not forgotten.

Through all this, I began to understand something deeper about faith. It wasn't just about showing up to church on Sundays or knowing scripture by heart. It was about going after the one lost sheep, the one who might feel like they had been left behind. Jesus left the ninety-nine to find the one, and I saw that principle in action every time we stepped into another home, another hospital room, another quiet space where someone was waiting for a reminder that they were seen, that they mattered.

That lesson stayed with me. It shaped how I approached ministry and service in ways I never expected.

On Sundays, before most people even arrived at church, he was already on the road, driving the youth Sunday school bus. The kids who climbed into that bus came from different backgrounds, some from homes where faith wasn't talked about at all. Yet, he greeted each one by name, asked about their week, and made sure they felt welcome before they even stepped through the church doors.

But his servanthood didn't stop there. He also led the adult Sunday school class. The same class that he would eventually ask me to lead. Leading a class filled with seniors who had been Christians for longer than I'd been alive was a challenging task. At the time, I was in my twenties, and here I was, leading people who had decades of wisdom. Despite being younger than many in the room, I approached the class with humility, never assuming I had all the answers. Instead, I made it a point to learn with the group, encouraging dialogue and growth. My spiritual mentor showed me that leadership wasn't about age or experience—it was about relationships, willingness to serve, and the humility to continue learning.

In everything he did, he exemplified what it means to have a faith that is active. His leadership, whether in teaching scripture or laying flooring in a new church gym, was a living testimony to the power of faith put into action. His example shaped me and many others, teaching me the power of loving those who may be at the end of their lives, helping shut-ins feel seen, and always, always going after that lost sheep. That is the heart of mentorship and ministry.

Personal Mentorship: Building Social Capital

Reader, I hope you recognize the importance of helping those struggling with poverty in building social capital. This refers to the relationships and cultural awareness that help individuals advance.

Growing up in the hollers and rarely leaving them, I had little opportunity to develop social capital. It hindered my chances of success. I remember joking with my brother about how poor we were growing up. He responded, "Yeah, but you made it out. Look at you now." His comment wasn't meant to be hurtful, but it struck a nerve. Look at me now? He saw what he viewed as someone who was successful, but not the struggle—the tears, the embarrassment, the lonely journey of learning hard lessons without guidance.

I have spent thousands of days investing in social capital—learning how and when to speak, what to wear, who to connect with, studying influence, etiquette, education, and professional behavior. Many are born into environments where these lessons come naturally, but I had to fight for every piece of knowledge. Once I reached the baseline of someone from a middle-class background, I could finally begin to build beyond it.

I am no longer intimidated by formal dinners—I know which fork to use. Meeting high-ranking officials no longer unsettles me—I know how to introduce myself with confidence. I no longer avoid cameras—I have learned to present myself well. These skills are essential in building the social capital and confidence necessary to break free from poverty.

These experiences have shown me that building social capital goes beyond personal achievements. It's about understanding how to interact with others and leverage those relationships for growth effectively.

While personal confidence is crucial, the true value lies in applying knowledge that leads to sustained progress. It's essential to recognize that building social capital isn't just about appearances, but rather making informed decisions and focusing on real, actionable steps.

While building social capital, I would advise against relying on mere opinions. Bridges Out of Poverty states that opinions are the lowest form of human knowledge; they require no accountability or true understanding[11]. Instead, focus on facts and proven techniques for upward mobility. Growth isn't about assumptions—it's about learning, adapting, and applying the right knowledge.

Proverbs 27:17 (KJV) Iron sharpeneth iron; so a man sharpeneth the countenance of his friend."

Chapter 12:

DIGNITY

D ignity is the state of being worthy of honor and respect. Without realizing it, many well-intentioned people, including churches worldwide, strip others of their dignity. I, too, have been guilty of this over the years.

A lesson I am constantly reminded of is not to do for my toddler what he can do for himself. If I always step in, I take away his chance to build confidence in his own abilities. The same principle applies to adults. When people are repeatedly placed in positions where they do not contribute to their own success, they begin to lose respect for themselves. Accomplishment fosters pride, and stripping away opportunities for people to achieve on their own can rob them of that pride.

The book *"When Helping Hurts"* illustrates this concept with a powerful example. Imagine a church that raises tens of thousands of dollars to send a group of volunteers to a developing country to build a house for a struggling family. The mission team arrives with good intentions, ready to make a difference. But as they hammer nails and lay bricks, middle-aged men from the same community stand on the sidelines, watching as privileged foreigners build a home for them. What message does this send? Instead of empowering these men to take charge of their own futures, it reinforces the idea that they are helpless and dependent on outside aid. This approach may feel productive at the moment, but it ultimately does more harm than good. If billions of dollars have been poured into eradicating global poverty, why have we made so little progress? Perhaps the problem lies in treating the symptoms rather than addressing the root causes. In the process, we are also unintentionally stripping people of their dignity.[12]

A more effective approach would be to provide these individuals with the tools, training, and encouragement to build their own homes. If the men and women in these communities were given the knowledge and resources to improve their own living conditions, the impact would be far greater reaching. Beyond meeting their immediate needs, they could gain the skills to support themselves long-term. Some might start businesses, create employment opportunities, and strengthen their local economies. The ripple effect could lead to lasting change. Yet, many volunteers struggle with this approach because it requires time, patience, and humility. It is far easier to spend two weeks on a mission trip, build something tangible, take pictures, and return home with a sense of accomplishment. But if the goal is real transformation, then the focus must shift from short-term relief to sustainable development.

This idea is not just relevant to mission work abroad; it applies to our own communities as well. Growing up, I attended church multiple times a week. It was where I learned valuable lessons and, most importantly, where I came to know Jesus. There was a wealthy man in my church who sat in front of me every Sunday. After giving his offering, he would casually slip a few dollars into my hand. To me, he was larger than life. We rarely saw cash at home, so those few dollars felt like treasure. Every week, I would rush to spend them on junk food, a luxury we could not afford otherwise.

Everyone in the church knew we were poor. They knew my grandparents had taken in my siblings and me. They knew our parents were battling addiction and mental illness. My grandparents often stood before the congregation, asking for prayers to help them carry the weight of raising us on their limited income.

Yet, looking back, I wonder—did those small acts of charity help me in the long run? Or did they subtly reinforce my own sense of dependence? There is a fine line between generosity and enabling. True dignity comes from being seen as capable, not pitied. People do not need a handout as much as they need a hand up. The greatest gift we can give others is the ability to stand on their own.

I do not doubt that the wealthy gentleman meant well. He probably went home feeling great about himself, convinced he had done a good deed. Over the years, he might have even shared the story of how he "helped" a poor kid at church. But what did he really do for me? Did he teach me anything? Equip me with tools to break free from my situation? Instill in me a sense of dignity? The answer is no.

This man influenced for years. He had opportunities for years. Yet, he never felt compelled to do more than offer a fleeting moment of charity.

I urge you, reader, not to make the same mistake. No matter how small it may seem, you have influence over someone. You have an opportunity to teach them to fish rather than simply handing them fish whenever you feel generous. It takes time, and there is no quick fix, but real change is possible.

Let me give you a smaller, more personal example of this.

At twenty-one, I was nearing the end of my undergraduate degree in sociology when one of my younger brothers was barely making it through high school. He was graduating by the skin of his teeth, having struggled academically for years. He had received a disability check his entire life. At some point, he began to watch me intentionally. He saw me pushing through poverty, earning a college education, and carving out a different path. If I could do it, he figured, maybe he could too.

He soon realized that the small disability check would never be enough for the kind of life he wanted. Determined to help, I petitioned the college leadership to grant him admission, even though he did not meet the academic requirements. I had built a decent reputation, and the school took a chance on him because he was my brother.

But years of neglecting his education had left him unprepared, and without strong role models in his immediate environment, he struggled to adjust. After just one semester, he was placed on academic probation. By the next, he was dismissed.

The experience strained our relationship. Heated arguments turned into silence, and for a couple of years, we barely spoke. Then, at twenty-seven, he reached out again, wanting more for his life.

For years, he had bounced between dead-end, minimum-wage jobs, working part-time and barely scraping by. He was still living with mamaw, still struggling, and still stuck in the same cycle. Worse, he was driving illegally without a license.

What he needed wasn't someone to give him a ride—he needed someone to teach him to drive.

So I did.

For weeks, my evenings and weekends were no longer mine. Instead of resting after long days, I spent hours preparing him for his driving test. It cost me time, energy, and money, but I never asked him for a dime. I drove him two counties over to practice the test course. Each session was a battle—not just against the technical skills required but against the years of self-doubt, anxiety, and depression that had built up inside him.

There were times he broke down, cursing, crying, convinced he would never be as good as me or as well-liked. One night, during one of these outbursts, he admitted that not long ago, he had tried to end his own life.

I reminded him, as I have many times before, that I am not better than him. God made us both in His image, and we each have our unique path. The enemy, the devil, had spent years convincing him of a lie, making him believe he was less than. But that is not the truth. We are both equally loved by God, equally capable of greatness, and no comparison can change that.

Sadly, my beloved brother had no dignity left.

It was at that moment that I felt God was giving me a chance to breathe dignity back into him. I told him he was loved, that he mattered, and that he was worthy—not just of a driver's license, but of stability, of independence, of a future. He didn't believe me at first. Years of feeling invisible had made those words impossible to accept. But each time I dropped him off, I hoped the weight of them would settle in.

Slowly, they did.

A few weeks later, he passed his test. No more driving illegally. No more uncertainty about how he would get to work. He even managed to get car insurance on his own. Together, we spent time finding him a used car, and for the first time, he was truly on his way to something better.

I don't share this story to pat myself on the back. I share it because this is what restoring dignity looks like. It's not a one-time gesture, nor a quick fix. It's a marathon, one that requires patience, sacrifice, and a deep commitment to investing in someone's future. It's about showing up consistently, understanding that the journey is long and the results may not be immediate, but the impact is profound. Restoring dignity isn't just about offering help in a moment of need; it's about walking alongside someone, empowering them, and creating a lasting change that will endure for years to come.

Proverbs 19:17 (KJV) "He that hath pity upon the poor lendeth unto the Lord; and that which he hath given will he pay him again."

Chapter 13:

F.R.E.E

May 10th is a date I'll always remember, not because of a personal milestone, but because of an event that profoundly shifted my perspective. I had traveled with a mentor to an event, a gathering of individuals from all across the state. Many of them were searching for direction, inspiration, or something more. My mentor wasn't the only speaker that day. Before he took the stage, a Senior Fellow from the American Enterprise Institute addressed the crowd. His title, though impressive, didn't move me. I had been surrounded by people with titles, such as professors, politicians, and executives, but it was his message that captured my attention.

It was during this talk that I first encountered the concept of F.R.E.E., a framework for upward mobility[13]. This wasn't just a catchy phrase; it became a roadmap for the work ahead. As he explained the components of F.R.E.E., I realized it was about much more than luck or circumstance. **F** stands for faith, the belief that with God's guidance, anything is possible, even when the road is uncertain. **R** is for resilience, the strength to persevere no matter how many times life knocks you down. **E** represents education, the key that unlocks doors to opportunities that would otherwise remain closed. And the last **E** stands for entrepreneurship, the power to build something of your own, to create jobs, and to impact your community in meaningful ways.

At that time, I was already in a season of deep reflection, growth, and understanding. I was refining my purpose, seeking clarity about the road ahead. A few weeks later, I would finalize my life's mission statement: to eliminate poverty in Appalachia while honoring my family.

By most standards, I had already achieved some worldly success. I had held a few job titles, earned a master's degree, and broken free from financial hardship. Yet, something was still missing. I wasn't searching for money or accolades. I was looking for meaning, for my true calling.

Throughout my journey, I have always believed in the importance of order, of doing things the right way, even when I stumbled. Time and time again, God redirected my steps, filling in the gaps where I couldn't see the way forward. While I didn't have an earthly family to guide me, I had God. I ran to my heavenly father for wisdom, and that truth shaped my path.

I am a first-generation high school graduate, the first in my family to attend college, and the first to earn a master's degree. Education didn't just change my life; it rewrote my family's story. It shattered generational cycles and created opportunities I never imagined. And then, there's the final piece of F.R.E.E., entrepreneurship.

Entrepreneurship is about building something of your own, taking an idea, nurturing it, and watching it grow. It's about creating jobs, contributing to your community, and paving your own path instead of waiting for permission. That is freedom, that is impact, and that is legacy.

As I listened to the speaker, the pieces of my own journey began to connect. F.R.E.E. is not just about titles or external achievements. It's about faith, resilience, education, and entrepreneurship, the very essence of upward mobility.

And for the first time in my life, I understood that I wasn't just free. I was called to help others find that same freedom.

Growing up, I always joked with friends about what kind of business we would build together. I would be the one making the big decisions while they handled the day-to-day operations. It was all talk back then, but deep down, I knew I wanted to create something of my own. I didn't know exactly what it would be, but I knew I didn't want to struggle forever. Looking back, I realize that my entrepreneurial spirit wasn't just a random dream. It was shaped by the lack of resources I experienced. When you grow up without much, you start thinking differently. You begin to see opportunities where others don't. You learn to make things work with what little you have. That mindset stuck with me.

At the time, I believed that if I could just make it out of my circumstances, I could accomplish something meaningful. I didn't have a clear plan, but I had determination. That drive pushed me to make better choices, even when temptation was everywhere. I had seen too many people fall into cycles they couldn't escape, and I didn't want that for myself.

One concept that stood out to me from the talk given by Senior Fellow Ian Rowe was his "success sequence." He explained that if a person waits until after high school to have children and gets married first, they have a 98 percent chance of avoiding poverty[12]. That number stayed with me. It made me think about how easily life could have gone another way. I had three pregnancy scares before I even graduated high school. Any one of them could have changed everything. I was young, reckless, and not thinking ahead.

But somehow, God had a different plan for me. It felt like He stepped in and shook me awake, making me realize that I needed to be more careful. I was supposed to build a better future for myself. I was meant to be with my childhood best friend, the one who had the same determination to break free from generational struggles. She had common sense, ambition, and a drive to do better. Being with her helped me stay focused, and together, we pushed each other to rise above the limitations placed on us.

Looking back, I am grateful for those moments of clarity. They kept me from making decisions that would have altered my future. They gave me the strength to stay on the path toward something greater. I know now that success isn't just about luck or talent. It's about choices. The right choices, made consistently, can shape the course of your life in ways you can't always see in the moment, but in the end, they make all the difference. Each decision, no matter how small it seems, has the power to move you closer to the life you're meant to live.

Psalm 119:105 (KJV) "Thy word is a lamp unto my feet, and a light unto my path."

Chapter 14:

THEY WERE ALL CLUES

I had a lot of friends who came from broken homes, but not all of them experienced poverty—at least not the kind that could be measured in dollars and cents. Some had parents who had split up, and some had grown up in chaotic households, but they still had stability in ways I could only imagine. They had a kind of life that felt so close yet so far from me, like a picture behind a glass frame that I could see but never touch.

I often found myself feeling like an outsider, staring through a frosted window at a family gathered around a warm fire. I wasn't part of the scene, just an observer, watching people experience things I had only ever dreamed of. There was a warmth in those homes that I had never known firsthand. Laughter that wasn't forced, conversations that didn't revolve around bills or survival. What was it like to have that? To know, without a doubt, that at the end of the day, you had a home to return to, parents who would be there, food on the table, and a bed that was yours alone?

I had always been fascinated by the idea of a "normal" family, though I didn't know what "normal" really meant. What was it like to have parents who were close to your age, who could relate to the world you lived in, instead of ones who seemed like they had already given up on dreaming? What was it like to have someone you could go to for advice without fear of judgment? Someone who would actually listen, not just tell you to toughen up and figure it out on your own?

What was it like to have parents who worked? I had never seen that. The adults around me were either unemployed, working odd jobs, or struggling to make ends meet in ways that always felt desperate. I would hear my friends talk about their parents' careers, about how their dad was an electrician or their mom worked in an office. It fascinated me. Not because I wanted to be an electrician or work in an office, but because it meant stability. It meant there was a plan, a routine, a life that wasn't dictated by the panic of making it through the week.

And then there were the small things—things most kids took for granted but felt like luxuries to me. What was it like to have money for fun things? Not just for rent, food, or whatever emergency popped up, but for things that had no purpose other than enjoyment. What was it like to go to the movies without calculating how much you'd have left afterward? To walk through the local county fair and actually participate instead of just looking at the rides and smelling the food you couldn't afford? What was it like to have an allowance? To know that money would come regularly, just for you, without having to fight for it?

I wondered about even smaller things, the ones that most people wouldn't even think about. What was it like to have your own space? Your own dresser? Your own toothbrush that no one else used? Your own stick of deodorant, your own razor, your own bed? Privacy wasn't a thing where I came from. Everything was shared, borrowed, or repurposed. If you had something nice, you guarded it because nothing stayed yours for long. I remember after I started cutting lawns and earning my own money, I would buy my pop and hide it from my family to keep them from consuming it all themselves or trying to sell it for alcohol or drugs.

What about parents who were involved? Not just ones who provided shelter and food when they could, but ones who actually cared about what you did with your life. What was it like to have parents who encouraged you to play sports, join clubs, to dream beyond your circumstances? What was it like to have a mom or dad who showed up to your games, cheered you on, and pushed you to do better because they saw something in you that you couldn't yet see in yourself?

I envied the kind of relationships my friends had with their parents—the way they could joke around, tease each other, even argue without fear. What was it like to have parents who asked about your dating life simply because they cared? What was it like to have a mom who reminded you to bring flowers to a girl on a first date or a dad who gave you advice about relationships?

But most of all, what was it like to have parents who wished you goodnight? Who checked on you before bed, tucked you in, and whispered that they loved you? What was it like to have someone pray for you, with you, reminding you that you were covered, protected, and wanted? I had seen glimpses of this in other homes, and each time, it left me feeling something I couldn't fully explain. Longing? Hope? Maybe both.

All these moments, all these observations, were clues. At the time, I didn't understand what they were leading me to, but I knew they meant something. I thought about them constantly, turning them over in my mind, comparing them to my own life, and wondering why things were so different. These weren't just questions— they were pieces of a puzzle I didn't yet know how to put together.

I didn't just want to escape poverty. I wanted to understand what made a life different. What made one person thrive while another struggled? What made a home warm, a family whole? And, more importantly, how could I create that for myself one day?

I carried these thoughts with me like a quiet whisper in the back of my mind. I watched. I listened. I paid attention to every detail, every difference between my life and the lives of those around me. And though I didn't realize it at the time, those clues were shaping me. They were guiding me, showing me a path that I hadn't even known existed.

I wasn't just observing. I was learning. And someday, I would take all those lessons, all those pieces, and build something different. Something better.

My Life's Mission

My life's mission is simple: to eliminate poverty in Appalachia while honoring my family.

That means success is not just about personal achievement. It is about making a difference without losing sight of where I came from or the people who shaped me. It means I refuse to chase my ambitions at the expense of those I love. It means I am committed to lifting others as I rise.

For years, I lived by this mission without ever putting it into words. I worked toward it without clearly defining it. I had a vision, but I had not named it. I was moving in the right direction, but without a target in front of me, I was just hoping to land somewhere close.

I remember speaking at a leadership conference when I was twenty-nine. The room was filled with Appalachian leaders, people in their thirties and forties who had worked hard to change their circumstances. I asked a simple question: "How many of you have a written life mission statement?"

There were forty-five people in that room. Only three hands went up. And I was one of them.

That moment was a wake-up call. It made me realize how many people break free from poverty, work their way to a better life, and then stop reaching. They feel because they are doing better than their parents did, they have done enough. And maybe that is true for them. But what about the lives they could still impact?

Most people spend the first thirty years of their lives trying to build something for themselves. If they manage to escape poverty, they feel relieved. But what about the next fifty years? That is a long time to just sit back and feel accomplished.

To me, success is not a finish line. It is a responsibility. If I can rise above the struggles I was born into, then I have an obligation to help others do the same. It is not just about my own comfort or stability. It is about creating opportunities for those who come after me.

I do not want to be someone who made it out and then looked away. I want to be someone who made it out and then turned around to pull others out of the miry clay of poverty. That is my mission. That is my purpose. And that is the life I will continue to build.

Picture decades of looking in the mirror, nodding in self-approval, and telling yourself, "I made it." But what if the real measure of success isn't just about making it out? What if it's about reaching back in? What if the real victory isn't in escaping poverty, but rather making sure fewer people get trapped in it in the first place?

I want you to take a moment—just one moment— and think about your life's mission. Not a to-do list. Not short-term goals. I'm talking about a sentence that will serve as your lighthouse, a sentence so powerful that it will guide every major decision you make. Something that will make you get up in the morning with a sense of direction, something that will keep you grounded when distractions pull at you from every side.

Here's the thing—you made it out. You climbed out of the struggle. You built a life where you're no longer drowning, gasping for air, hoping for a lifeline. You've broken a cycle. And that is worth celebrating. But if your only takeaway from that journey is personal relief, you've missed the bigger picture.

Poverty isn't just about lacking money. It's an invisible chain, dragging people down generation after generation. It feeds hopelessness. It pushes people into desperation. It lures them into the arms of addiction. It turns dreams into regrets before they ever get the chance to grow. And when no one extends a hand, when no one reaches in to help, people don't just stay poor—they spiral.

I challenge you—grab their hand before it is too late. That is my life's mission. What is yours?

Maybe you don't know yet. Maybe you're still figuring it out. That's okay. But don't waste time wandering. Find someone a little wiser, a little older. Someone who has lived long enough to understand the weight of decisions. Someone who has a detailed plan and is willing to help you shape yours.

That is what I did. I was not too proud to admit that I needed guidance. I needed someone to teach me what I didn't yet know. And I found that person—not in the places where people sit around waiting for life to happen to them, but in the places where people make life happen.

The right people are out there. They are the ones with gray hairs, not the twenty-five-year-olds with trendy dye jobs and temporary wisdom. They are the ones with wrinkles, not from stress but from years of learning, growing, and enduring. They are found in churches, in schools, and in businesses. They are the ones who have built something with their lives, and more often than not, they are looking for someone to invest in.

And here's the thing about investments—they aren't always about money. Some of the most valuable investments are made in people. In time. In knowledge. In mentorship. In reaching back and saying, "Let me show you the way."

I am not writing this as someone who has had it all figured out from the beginning. I am writing this as someone who once felt like he was barely keeping his head above water. Someone who was drowning, looking around, waiting, hoping, praying that someone would see me and pull me up before it was too late.

And because someone did, I am here. And because I am here, I refuse to forget what it felt like to be there.

Be that hand for someone else. Be the person who doesn't just escape the fire but goes back in to help those still trapped. That is what real success looks like. That is a mission worth living for.

As I mentioned before, I was a capable child. I got the good grades. I mostly stayed away from trouble. I didn't fall into the traps that swallowed so many others. Even with capability, I lacked one thing: guidance. And just because I didn't have it didn't mean I didn't crave it. I did. Desperately.

I wasn't searching for someone to hand me success. I wasn't looking for a shortcut. I just knew that if I had even a little direction, even a small push in the right way, I could do something meaningful. Not the flashy kind of success that makes for good TV, but the kind that changes a family tree. The kind that breaks cycles. The kind that ensures the next generation doesn't have to start from scratch. That is the intention of this book, *Me and Poverty*. MAP for short. It has been written to act as a roadmap to help others escape poverty. I encourage you to take this roadmap and use it to guide someone in your circle of influence to a brighter future.

I could make a decent living. I could be a strong, present father, the kind I never had. I could be a devoted husband, a supportive brother, a son my mother could be proud of. I knew I had it in me. I just needed someone to show me how. Please be that someone to somebody.

That lack of guidance shaped me. It left gaps in my foundation, places where doubt could creep in. Yet it also gave me a resolve, one that runs so deep it is now part of who I am. My son will never feel the same voids I did. He will never have to wonder if someone is there for him or if he is loved. I may not always get it right. I may stumble, and I may fail. But one thing is certain. I will always be there.

Chapter 15:

FAMILY MATTERS

A Father's Advice

H ello, my son. What a joy it is to call you that.

I thank God every day for allowing your mother and me to watch over you, to raise you, and guide you in the way you should go. It is a privilege, one I do not take lightly. I hope that as you grow, you see me as a loving and caring father. I hope you can say you found me faithful; faithful to God, faithful to your mother, and faithful to you. More than anything, I pray that you come to know Jesus more deeply than I ever have. However, that may not be easy. You see, son, He was all I had.

You, on the other hand, have a family that loves you beyond words, beyond reason, beyond even their next breath. Please, never take that for granted.

Because of my determination and the grace of God, you will have opportunities I never had. But with that comes distractions. I encourage you to find joy in the simple things. Love God, love yourself, and love others. Growing up; love, affection, and purpose were foreign concepts to me. They were things I had to learn later in life. I pray they are constants in yours, woven into your days, impossible to miss.

I hope you never experience the struggles I did. The doubts, the shame, the poverty, the fears, these are just a glimpse of the battles I fought. These things ran in our family for generations. That is, until they ran into me and God. And yes, I say that with pride. Not a selfish kind of pride, but the pride of a man who finally found a drink of water after wandering through the desert for far too long. The pride of someone who dared to change the course of his family tree.

I pray that the opportunities before you will not just serve you but will propel you forward beyond anything I have accomplished. I pray that your impact reaches further and that your life is a light expanding God's kingdom in ways I could only dream of.

A few guiding thoughts have shaped my journey, and I pray they serve you well too.

First, always remember that you are a spiritual being navigating a physical world, not the other way around. Your body is temporary, but your spirit is eternal. Never let the limitations of the flesh define the boundlessness of your soul. Second, we never say we can't. Challenges will come, but they are only obstacles if you let them be. See them as lessons, as stepping stones rather than barriers. Third, never throw away your shot. Never be afraid to take chances. In fact, chase them. Opportunities are often disguised as hard work, uncertainty, or even failure. Recognize them, seize them, and use them to propel yourself forward. Fourth, God has brought me this far for a reason, and I must ask myself daily—am I serving my life's mission? Are my actions aligned with the purpose He has set before me? Lastly, true growth and success are often found just beyond the edge of your comfort zone. If something feels difficult or intimidating, that may be the very thing you need to pursue.

There are countless other lessons worth sharing, but if you take nothing else from me, take this—we live in the world, but we are not of the world. That means you will be different. You will be called to stand apart, to walk a path that others may not understand. And that is okay.

When I was younger, I was ridiculed for wanting to be different. For daring to dream beyond what my immediate family could see. I grew up feeling out of place, lonely, and often abandoned. I carried that weight until my relationship with God became the foundation of my life. The closer I walked with Him, the less alone I felt. He became my source of strength, my refuge, my counselor when I had no one else to turn to. And as long as you honor God and act in love, you will never truly be alone either. The world may question your choices. People may misunderstand your vision. But if you are walking in alignment with God, you will always be exactly where you are meant to be.

Solitude taught me something important. Being alone does not mean being lonely. There is a difference. One isolates, and the other empowers. I learned to be comfortable in solitude because I knew I was never truly alone. God was with me every step of the way. He watched over me. He loved me. He protected me. And He guided me in ways that I only now realize. Any success I have in this world is because of Him, not because of my own merit, but because He made a way where there was none.

Life is short. Compared to eternity, our years on this earth are nothing more than a blink in time. So, focus on what truly matters. Ask yourself daily—what am I doing today that will impact someone forever? How am I contributing to the kingdom of God? You may be the only Bible someone ever reads. Let them see Jesus in you. Let your words, your actions, and your presence be a reflection of His love.

At the same time, life is also about balance, and I have struggled to find that. Let me be clear—your relationship with Christ is not about balance. It is about surrender. Complete, wholehearted, nothing-held-back surrender to the one true God. But in other areas of life, balance is key. It took me years to understand that success is not just about working hard; it is also about knowing when to step back, when to be present, and when to cherish the moments that cannot be recreated.

My life's mission has always been to eliminate poverty in Appalachia while honoring my family. That mission has shaped my choices, my sacrifices, and my prayers. But as I pursued that calling, I realized something important. Even the greatest mission is meaningless if it comes at the cost of the people who matter most. I never wanted my ambition to steal me away from my family. I never wanted success to mean absence. So I fought to be present, to be the kind of father you could look up to, not just in words but in action.

If there is anything I can leave with you, it is this: live with purpose, love deeply, and never lose sight of what is eternal. This world is fleeting, but what you do for God will last forever. Let your actions be guided by faith, your heart filled with compassion, and your life focused on the greater purpose that transcends time. In the end, it's not what you accumulate or achieve here that matters, but rather the love, service to others, and the eternal impact that ripples through the lives you touch that matters most.

Honoring My Wife

What a journey we have been on. Through every season, through struggles and victories, through uncertainty and growth, you have been my constant. Thank you for loving me despite my poverty. Thank you for seeing beyond the lack and into the man I could become. Thank you for taking a chance on a kid with too many rough edges and for choosing to stand beside me when it would have been easier to walk away.

You looked past my unfortunate family situation, never letting it define how you saw me. You never made me feel ashamed of where I came from, even when I carried that shame myself. You put up with my anger, my frustrations, and my moments of doubt. You saw something in me that I couldn't always see in myself. You believed in me when I had no reason to believe in myself. Maybe most of all, thank you for finding me worthy of love, not because I had done anything to deserve it, but because you gave it freely. What a picture of Christ's love in action. That has certainly shaped me into the man I am today.

You were always there, always my biggest fan, always my greatest encourager. We pushed each other, challenged each other, and even competed academically. I remember how I used to downplay my intelligence, trying to balance the fine line between smart and cool. I never wanted to appear like I was trying too hard, but the truth is, I admired you. I admired your boldness, your dedication, and the way you took your education seriously when I was too distracted to care. You never let anyone dim your light. You never pretended to be less than who you were, and I respected that.

When I nearly threw my entire future away, it was you who spoke sense into me. Your words cut through the noise; your belief in me carried weight. I do not know where I would be today if not for you. I do not know if I would have had the courage to turn things around. You saw potential in me long before I ever proved myself. You saw my heart when I only saw my failures.

I also admired something else about you, something I never had growing up. You had parents who were present. They were overbearing at times, sure, but they were there. Watching, guiding, protecting. That kind of stability was foreign to me. I used to wonder what it would have been like to grow up in a home like that, to have parents who set expectations, who reminded you that you were loved, who showed up for every milestone. I did not have that. I had to figure a lot out on my own. But because of you, I saw the difference it made. And now, as we raise a child of our own, I understand it in a way I never could before. I see the weight of responsibility. I see how much presence matters. I see how small moments shape a child's future.

I write this chapter to honor you, my wife, my best friend, because my life's mission has always been clear. To eliminate poverty in Appalachia while honoring my family. You are my family. You are the heart of it all. You are the one who made everything feel possible. But I also write this for anyone who may be wondering what kind of partner to wait for and what kind of love to seek. This decision carries so much weight. Second, only to deciding to follow Christ.

I once received a piece of advice that has stayed with me to this day. You are supposed to marry your best friend.

I can proudly say I did. And I thank God for it every single day.

I will always admire your patience, Daisha. You waited for me, even when I didn't deserve it. You watched me stumble through my own stupidity, making mistakes, chasing the wrong things, and being reckless with my own future. You sat back, never judging, never pushing, just waiting. You were always there, always steady, always my friend. Never forceful, always kind. Always caring.

Thank you for demanding grade school hugs in the hall between classes, no matter who I may have been "dating" at the time. You didn't care about the eyes watching or the whispers around us. You just cared about me. Thank you for listening when I needed to talk and for being the one person I could always count on. Thank you for the shoulder to lean on, the unwavering support, and the effortless way you made everything feel a little lighter. You were the warmth I needed on days when everything felt cold. You were the rays of sun that broke through my darkest moments.

When I felt I had no worth, God sent you to remind me I was worthy of being loved. I will never forget the eighth-grade awards night. I wasn't going to go. Not because I didn't want to, but because my grandparents didn't see the point, and that meant I had no ride. To them, it wasn't significant. But to me, it was another reminder of how alone I often felt.

You volunteered to take me even against your mother's wishes. She didn't like me. She made that clear. I can't say I blamed her. She wanted better for you, wanted you to have a crush on someone with a "normal" family. Someone who didn't come from poverty. Someone who didn't walk into every event smelling like cigarette smoke, like the very thing I tried so hard to escape. Someone who had at least one person in their family who cared enough to bring them to something as simple as an academic awards banquet. She simply wanted to protect you, having our son now, I can understand.

And the truth? I wanted better for you too. I never felt like I deserved someone as kind, as loving, as steady as you. That's why it took me so long to wake up and ask you to be my girlfriend the summer before our senior year of high school. It wasn't just my own foolishness holding me back—it was the belief that you deserved someone who wasn't me.

Back to awards night...I remember walking into the ceremony, feeling like I didn't belong. Like I was just another kid no one expected much from. And then they started calling names, handing out awards. One after another. And somehow, despite everything, I ended up receiving more awards than you. I still remember the look on your mother's face—shocked that someone like me could be doing so well while carrying the weight of a broken home.

Thank you for that car ride. Thank you for showing up when no one else did. That night, for the first time in a long time, I felt a sliver of hope. A small but powerful reminder that maybe, just maybe, I could make it out.

At the beginning of this chapter, I referred to our journey. Looking back, much of it was carefully planned, and mapped out long before we ever reached each milestone. I always knew I wanted to be the kind of father I never had. I wanted to break the cycle, to give my children the love, stability, and guidance that had been missing from my own childhood. But unlike the rest of my family, I also knew I didn't want to have children too soon. I had a plan. No children until I was twenty-six. And when did we have our son? At twenty-six.

Thank you for the gift of our boy. Through every long night, every moment of doubt, every challenge that made us question if we were doing enough, one thing has always been certain. We are good, loving parents. He may just stand a chance in this crazy world because of that.

We dated for a few years before getting engaged during college. I remember those years so vividly, the late nights, the shared dreams, and the quiet understanding that we were building something real. Our bucket list from back then is still proof today. I worked sixteen-hour days during the summers and winters, pushing through exhaustion, and saving every penny for that engagement ring. I was determined to do it the right way, to earn it, to give you something that reflected even a fraction of what you meant to me. And yes, I am proud of that. You were so worth it.

Six months after graduating with our bachelor's degrees, we were married. That was another decision we made with intention. We wanted a strong foundation, something built on commitment, faith, and mutual respect. Even our textbooks reinforced what we already believed—contrary to popular opinion, couples who cohabitate before marriage have a higher divorce rate. It was a statistic that stood out, one we couldn't ignore. And so, we waited. We rented a house together, but you didn't move in until after we were married. It wasn't always easy, but it was right for us.

We sure didn't have much straight out of school. In fact, for the first few years, I was pretty frustrated by how little money we had after pouring three and a half years of our lives into what felt like a useless degree. I remember our first Valentine's Day out of college, sitting on the dining room floor because we couldn't afford a table yet, eating cheap spaghetti surrounded by rose petals and candles. It was simple, maybe even a little ridiculous, but it was ours. We made the most of what we had, and somehow, that made it enough.

I often laugh at how easy it is to forget just how bad poverty was for me growing up. Every now and then, the past finds a way to remind me. A smell, a moment, a sudden wave of insecurity that lingers longer than it should. I still struggle with the damage it left behind. But those reminders also bring a truth I hold onto tightly—I get to be the husband I never witnessed growing up. I get to be the father I never had.

And for any success I have in either role, I credit you. I truly don't know where I would be without you. You have been my anchor, my partner, my constant when life has felt anything but steady. I thank God for you every single day. I thank Him for blessing us with a foundation strong enough to build a life upon, one rooted in biblical truth, love, and genuine friendship.

Thank you for being everything I never thought I deserved.

Reader, I encourage you to help others find the same. We are not meant to live this life alone and isolated. Help them find a love that strengthens them, that lifts them higher, that reminds them of what is good and true. Find a foundation that can withstand the weight of life because when the storms come, and they will, it is the strength of that foundation that will hold them together.

Ecclesiastes 4:9-12 (KJV) "Two are better than one; because they have a good reward for their labour. For if they fall, the one will lift up his fellow: but woe to him that is alone when he falleth; for he hath not another to help him up. Again, if two lie together, then they have heat: but how can one be warm alone? And if one prevail against him, two shall withstand him; and a threefold cord is not quickly broken."

THE END

ACKNOWLEDGMENTS

To my incredible Kickstarter backers:

Your belief in this project and your generous contributions toward covering the self-publishing costs have breathed life into every page of this book. Because of your support, "Me and Poverty" exists not just as words on a page but as a living roadmap for anyone seeking to navigate their way out of hardship. I am humbled by your faith, encouraged by your partnership, and honored to share this journey with you. May the story we've created together inspire others to chart their own course toward hope and freedom.

With deepest gratitude,
Joseph Little

Below is the list of the amazing backers whose generosity made this book possible:

Vadis and Teresa Gauze

Anthoney Spence

Corey Cassell

Friends of Odyssey

The Ash Family

Thomas Case

Kara Stanton

The Osborn Family

David Walker Jr.

Juanita Porter

Andrea Muncy

Courtney Howell

Joshua Moore

Marcie Ward Hanson

Emily Stanley

Adele Newman

Angela Clevenger

Collan and Bre McCoy

Aleigh Horn

The Goforth Family

Brian Davis

Courtney Smith

Ashlee Sizemore

Kara Stanton

Stephan Harris

John Barker

Thomas Case

Jeanette Burke

Wes Kingsmore

Tom Bradley

Brittany Blevins

Heath Bootle

Adam Rucker

The Mollett Family

Curt and Judy Fitzpatrick

Vicky Mayhan

ADDITIONAL RESOURCES & NEXT STEPS

Thank you for reading *Me and Poverty: A Journey of Inspiration and Escape*. Your journey doesn't have to end here—explore the resources below to stay connected, keep growing, and help others break free from hardship.

1. Join the Newsletter
Stay up-to-date on new blog posts, exclusive excerpts, and writing insights. Sign up at my website: https://www.joelittleinspires.com/

2. Subscribe on YouTube
Hear more of my story, discover inspiring journeys of others, and grab practical pit stops for mentors and youth-support professionals. Subscribe at: https://youtube.com/@meandpoverty?si=qKzyJSZGVL wuTI1Q

3. Listen or Watch the Podcast

Me and Poverty is available on Spotify and Apple Podcasts. Tune in for weekly conversations with guests who share tools and hope for overcoming challenges:

- Spotify: [Search "Me and Poverty" in the Spotify app]
- Apple Podcasts: [Search "Me and Poverty" in the Apple Podcasts app]

4. Book a Speaking Event

Bring an interactive workshop or keynote to your organization, school, or conference. Visit my website and use the contact form to request availability and discuss your needs:

https://www.joelittleinspires.com/

5. Bulk Order Discounts

Interested in purchasing copies for your class, youth group, or organization? Email me through the contact form on my website for special rates on large orders.

6. Leave a Review

If *Me and Poverty* has inspired you, please consider posting a brief review on Amazon or Goodreads. Your feedback helps others find the book and keeps the conversation going.

Each step you take, and every person you share this book with, helps build a roadmap out of poverty for individuals and families. Thank you for being part of this mission—let's keep navigating toward hope, dignity, and lasting change.

ENDNOTES

1. Wiest, B. (2020). *The mountain is you: Transforming self-sabotage into self-mastery.* Thought Catalog Books.

2. Johnson, L. B. (1964, April 24). *Remarks in Inez, Kentucky: War on poverty speech.* The American Presidency Project. Retrieved from https://www.presidency.ucsb.edu

3. Appalachian Regional Commission. (2023). *Income and poverty in Appalachia.* Retrieved from https://www.arc.gov

4. Federal Reserve Bank of Atlanta. (n.d.). *What are benefits cliffs?* Retrieved from https://www.atlantafed.org

5. Hendricks, G. (2009). *The big leap: Conquer your hidden fear and take life to the next level.* HarperOne.

6. Miranda, L.-M. (2015). My shot [Song]. On *Hamilton: An American Musical.* Atlantic Records.

7. Elmore, A. L., & Clements, P. T. (2021). *Bereavement and heart disease risks.* Futurity. Retrieved March 25, 2025, from https://www.futurity.org/bereavement-heart-disease-risks-1744992/

8. Clear, J. (2018). *Atomic Habits: An Easy and Proven Way to Build Good Habits & Break Bad Ones.* Avery, an Imprint of Penguin Random House

9. Maslow, A. H. (1943). *A theory of human motivation.* Psychological Review, 50(4), 370–396. https://doi.org/10.1037/h0054346

10. Collins, J. (2001). *Good to Great: Why Some Companies Make the Leap...and Others Don't.* Harper Collins

11. Payne, R. K., DeVol, P. E., & Smith, T. D. (2001). *Bridges Out of Poverty: Strategies for Professionals and Communities.* aha! Process, Inc.

12. Corbett, S., & Fikkert, B. (2009). *When Helping Hurts: How to Alleviate Poverty Without Hurting the Poor... and Yourself.* Moody Publishers.

13. Rowe, I. (2022). Agency: The *Four Point Plan (F.R.E.E.) for All Children to Overcome the Victimhood Narrative and Discover Their Pathway to Power.* Templeton Press.

www.ingramcontent.com/pod-product-compliance
Lightning Source LLC
Chambersburg PA
CBHW060127130626
46556CB00006B/2255